TEACHING EFFECTIV
RELATION TO ORGANIZATIONAL CLIMATE, MENTAL
HEALTH AND ATTITUDE TOWARDS INFORMATION
AND COMMUNICATION TECHNOLOGY (ICT)

TRISHNA DEVI

CONTENTS

Page No.

Certificate	
Declaration	ii
Acknowledgement	iii-v
Preface	vi-viii
Contents	ix-xii
List of Figures	xiii-xiv
List of Tables	xv-xviii
Abbreviations	xix

CHAPTER-I: INTRODUCTION 1-56

Section A: Context of the study	1
Section B: Key Concepts of the Study and Theoretical Framework	3
B.1 Conceptualizing Teaching Effectiveness	4
B.2 Models of Teaching Effectiveness	8
B.2 (i) Hay McBer Model of Teaching Effectiveness (2000)	8
B.2 (ii) Clark and Walsh's (2002) Model of Effective Teacher	11
B.2 (iii) Teaching Effectiveness Model of Robert Marzano's (2012)	11
B.3 Organizational climate as a multifaceted (multidimensional) set up	12
B.3 (i) Dimensions influencing organizational climate	15
B.3 (ii) Models comprising parameters of organizational climate	18
B.4 Mental health as a challenge in workplace	21
B.4 (i) Dimensions of mental health	24

B.4 (ii)	Mental health scenario of teachers	26
B.5	ICT and teacher attitude	28
B.5 (i)	ICT as a Changing Agent in Higher Education	31
B.5 (ii)	Models of ICT	34
B.5 (ii) (a)	TPACK Model (Technological Pedagogical Content Knowledge)	34
B.5 (ii) (b)	Unified Theory of Acceptance and Use of Technology (TUAUT)	36
B.5 (iii)	Notable initiatives for implementing ICT in Indian edu. landscape	37

Section C: Conceptualization of the study		41
C.1	Statement of the problem	41
C.2	Research Questions	43
C.3	Research Objectives	43
C.4	Hypotheses of the Study	44
C.5	Significance of the study	46
C.6	Scope of the study	51
C.7	Proposed model of the study	52
C.8	Operational definitions of the key concepts	53

CHAPTER-II: REVIEW OF LITERATURE   57-94

CAHPETER-III: RESEARCH METHODOLOGY   95-122

3.1	Introduction	95
3.2	Research method	95
3.3	Geographical coverage	97
3.4	Description of population and sample	99
	3.4.1 Population of the study	99
	3.4.2 Sample size	100

	3.4.2 (A) Criteria for selection of sample		103
	3.4.2 (B) Source of data and criteria for selection of college		104
	3.4.2 (C) Sampling Technique		104
3.5	Research design		105
3.6	Variable under study		106
3.7	Data collection		107
	3.7.1	Procedure of primary data collection	107
	3.7.2	Secondary data collection	108
3.8	Description of the tools		109
	3.8.1	Teacher Effectiveness Scale	110
	3.8.2	General description of Organizational Climate Questionnaire	112
	3.8.3	Employee's Mental Health Inventory	115
	3.8.4	General description of Attitude towards ICT Questionnaire	117
3.9	Statistical techniques used for the present study		120
3.10	Ethical issues considered		121

CHAPTER-IV: RESULT AND DISCUSSION   123-192

4.1	Introduction	123
4.2	Descriptive Statistical Analysis	124
4.3	ONE-WAY ANOVA followed by TUCKEY'S HSD test	132
4.4	Correlation Analysis	167
4.4	Regression Analysis	187
4.5	Hypotheses Verification	189
4.6	An Overview of the Results	191

CHAPTER-V: SUMMARY, FINDINGS AND SUGGESTIONS 193-212

5.1	Summary	193
5.2	Findings of the study	201
5.3	Implications & recommendations for practices	207
5.4	Limitations of the study	209
5.5	Suggestions for further research	210
5.6	Conclusion	211

CHAPTER: 1
INTRODUCTION

This chapter contains three sections. Section **A** describes the context of the study, followed by Section B which is an introduction to the key terms used in the study. Finally, Section C depicts the conceptualization of the study.

Section A: Context of the study

"Teachers' place in society is of vital importance. He acts as the point of transmission of intellectual tradition and technical skill from generation to generation and helps to keep the lamp of civilization burning."- Dr. S. Radhakrishnan

In the present era of modernization, tremendous changes have been witnessed in every field. And, to adjust with the varying challenges in society, education is highlighted as one of the most potent instruments of imparting knowledge in different areas. Expeditious and extensive integration of scientific elaboration has transformed the current milieu. New advancements in technology prompted their potential role increasingly by providing enormous cognizance of existing content in the educational endeavour. Undoubtedly, the teacher is considered as the epical experienced person in the process of instructional shrine for moulding future citizens. It is generally agreed that enlightenment and empowerment of human being is very much dependant on the efficient teachers. As a consequence, it is cardinal for educators to integrate both professional and personal skills for maintaining new and challenging roles in teaching-learning activities. Due to the utmost possession of multitasks and paradoxical demands, teachers may have to discharge innumerable advanced provocation. And for achieving this, they require additional efforts apart from contributing conventional instructions to the students. So, the effectiveness of the teacher has become a matter of great concern in this regard. Whence, they should be sufficiently competent in handling the new millennium and also continues to bear ultimate strain relating to the strenuous teaching profession.

It is seen that teachers undergo heterogeneous contributions in both the internal and external surroundings of the organization. It is impossible to manage any organizational climate without ingenious execution. Generally, the climate of the organization is regarded as a multidimensional collective perception of the existing work environment. In the entire process of pedagogical endeavour, teachers' attribution and persuasion are of prominent importance which is influenced by the organizational climate. An essential point for notation is that the behaviour and outlooks of the members are affected by the climate within an organization **(Lin & Lee, 2017)**. Therefore, it is quite obvious to establish a favourable and healthy organizational setting. It is one of the most essential aspects to strengthen the organizational climate for efficient performance and innovativeness of teachers. Indeed, the conducive climate will bring overall quality based surroundings. Hence, there is an utmost attempt to accommodate a positive climate that can contribute creativity, energetic behaviour and attitude for continuous professional development.

Teaching effectiveness covers different domains that are linked to academic activities, such as interpersonal relations, classroom management ability, accomplishment in their subject-matter, etc. The role of good psychosocial health, along with inter alia, plays a pertinent role in this regard. In the present day context, mental health issues of educators act as a threatening issue in many countries. It has been stated in the **National Institute of Mental Health & Neurosciences (NIMHANS)** report that, more than 300 million people suffer from depression in India. Moreover, 260 million have anxiety disorders. This report carries a scandalous pervasiveness of mental sickness in India. So, there is the predominant necessity for proper awareness to lessen the mental illness. Although the perceived states of teaching effectiveness are subjective, it is the basis of some other associated aspects within the organization. These aspects are directly connected with the mental and physical health of the educators. So, for effectiveness, it is pre-requisite to remaining free from all mental and physical strain in any organizational setup.

Again, in this technologically advanced 21st century, teachers have to use information technology in every sphere of academic activities. In the present day context, the use of technologies is indispensable for all educational realm. The teacher faces a new challenge to cope up with the most promising, innovative pedagogical practices to build meaningful activities and sustainable learning experiences in the organization. Also, the effective application of technological advancements in the teaching processes largely depends on the knowledge of the user **(Aina, 2013).** According to **UNESCO (2008)**, effective teachers should have a firm knowledge of curriculum and also apply technological strategy into the curriculum. Therefore, it elicits a scope for the conviction that the utilization of information technology may subsequently lead to an influence on the academic achievement of a student.

Section B: Key Concepts of the Study and Theoretical Framework

In this study, four variables, namely, Teaching Effectiveness, Organisational Climate, Mental Health and Attitude towards Information and Communication Technology (ICT) are chosen as key points of the study. These are brought into the discussion, in chronological order, in section B.

B.1. Conceptualizing Teaching Effectiveness:

Predominantly, the term teaching is accepted as a challenging millennium as it focussed on paramount importance to come up with quality education. The major goal of instructional practices is to certify purposeful learning to bring about desirable change in learners. Quality with quantity and equity is related to every sphere of good teaching or teaching effectiveness. Effectiveness can also describe from diverse perspectives. Teaching Effectiveness refers specifically to the perfection characteristics of a teacher and in the teaching profession. However, teaching effectiveness or effective teaching is an already prevailing domain for investigation. Different critics and researchers have undertaken to explain the term "Teaching Effectiveness" in plentiful approaches along with their studies. Yet, due to diverse conception, it is not facile to give an accurate definition of teaching effectiveness. Although there exist some controversy and complex issues regarding teaching effectiveness, still it covers wide dimensions in diverse fields.

In the existing study, the researcher applied the term **"Teacher Effectiveness"** and **"Teaching Effectiveness"** in an interchanging manner with each other. The term **'Teaching Effectiveness'** implies the effectiveness of teaching with a broader goal to attain learning objectives, whereas the word **'Teacher Effectiveness'** assigns to the individual performance of the teacher. Teaching effectiveness for our purpose is concerned with the involvement of teachers in the classroom with an effort to persuade the students learning condition. Another essential aspect is that teaching effectiveness is not limited only to classroom activities as it refers to the overall effectiveness of teachers including other instructional areas. So, in the current study, the phrase teaching effectiveness, teacher effectiveness, teacher efficacy are used reciprocally due to the acceptance that teachers' ideas and activities do not occur any vacuity in teaching.

Evans (2006) has noted Teaching Effective in terms of three basic ways-

a) The personality of the teacher
b) Coordinate interaction with students and
c) Impact of teachers on students' behaviour.

So, it can be clearly stated that for maximization of students' academic attainment, the teacher-student relationship in carrying out the academic endeavour is of course satisfaction as a whole. Another crucial aspect that has received significant interest in the domain of effective teaching is the excellence attribute towards quality education **(Borkar, 2013)**. It is such an aspect that can enhance students learning and academic productivity in the entire system of education. Teaching effectiveness is also expected as the ways of planning, knowledge of content, preparation, presentation and the classroom interaction which will be related to creative activities in the classroom **(Wenglinsky, 2000)**.

Ansari & Ansari (2000) conceptualized teaching effectiveness as the person's both cognitive and non-cognitive attributes (like academic qualification and distinctions, clarity of thought and expression, fluency, teaching strategy, etc.) to organize and execute a required course of action to achieve the desired result. According to them, these attributes constitute the key factor of human agency. Effectiveness related ability is one of the most powerful characteristics associated with student's physical, intellectual and psychological interests to face difficulties of life (Dictionary of Education 2005) **[Kaur & Sharma, 2015]**. Teachers need to have increased effectiveness in teaching to bring the desired changes in the students' behaviour and this would pave the way for carrying out academic pursuits.

It is well documented by **Woolfolk (2004)** that "Teachers' knowledge, clarity, organization, warmth, and enthusiasm" are the core elements in explaining "effective teachers". A person with high effectiveness manipulates students to inculcate with positive self-confidence and self-satisfaction towards tremendous instructional aspects. Teaching related competency is one of the most powerful characteristics associated with a positive professional attitude, positive thinking, enthusiastic activities, better reciprocal interaction with colleagues and students **(Ahmad, Said, Zeb, Sihatullah & Rehman, 2013)**. It influences students' performance for carrying out a task with determination. Research suggests that teachers' efficacy is an antecedent of teachers' classroom behaviour, knowledge of subject-matter and instruction style, and teachers' beliefs on pupil learning **(Wray, Medwell, Fox & Poulson, 2000)**.

Teacher effectiveness is regarded as a multi-dimensional construct, consisting of various elements of the profession. **Anderson (2004)** has suggested that effective teaching is not important entirely on the cognizance and affective occurrence of teachers but also their overall integration of ability, knowledge, and personality as well. If the teacher competently takes an effort of the entire factors, then their effectiveness falls up to the optimal extent. **Aina & Adedo (2013)** found that feedback taking is very crucial in teaching to improve students' learning. Every effective teacher must have the proper knowledge of providing feedback and assessment among students. Although assessment activities take much time, it has an unavoidable existence in improving learning situation.

The perspective of an effective teacher is the subjective term and that has different strategies for assessing their attributes. **Glass (2011)** conceptualized effective teachers as planner, supervisor and also evaluator by using multiple sources of manifestation, which promote an efficient classroom environment. The research suggested that to be an effective teacher is a complex process **(Ru**bio**, 2009**; **Verma, 2016)**.Therefore, it can be said that personal qualities have a high perspective to influence the performance of teachers. **Day (2004)** has supported that the inherent qualities of the teacher are the prime and efficient factors in good teaching. Further, **Stronge (2007, p.22)** in his book *"Qualities of effective teacher",* emphasize the teachers' non-cognitive traits such as societal and emotive behaviours, more than didactic practices. More recently, **Chowdhury (2014)** emphasized that along with content and pedagogy there is an utmost necessity to unite life skills training (such as compassion, mutual relationship, abstract thinking, making decisions, coping with emotions and stress) with teaching and learning practices. Besides, personal qualities; to stimulate activities, frequent assessment and feedback, favourable physical-mental health and influential classroom atmosphere, etc. are must necessary during teaching **(Ko, et al. 2013)**. In this respect to recline desired direction teachers psychological, methodological, and philosophical as well as a physical state of consequences should give prominent importance. So, teaching effectiveness of a teacher is not only assessed from the academic pursuance but also from the total influence exerted by them upon the students. In a nutshell, the word 'teaching effectiveness' possesses a vast repository as there are many different conceptions of assessing the effectiveness of the teacher.

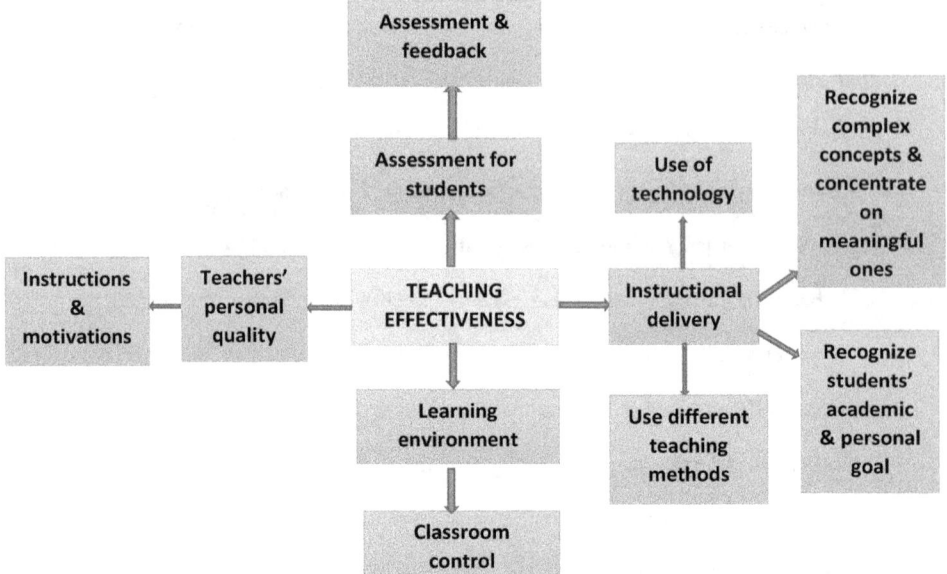

Fig.B.1: Conceptual framework of teaching effectiveness

B.2. Models of Teaching Effectiveness:

(i) Hay McBer Model of Teaching Effectiveness (2000): (Verma, 2016)

McBer (2000) postulates three distinctive factors to be of practical use to teachers for making teaching a more effective manner. His model confirms these three attributes:

a)   Professional characteristics

b)   Teaching skills and

c)   Classroom climate

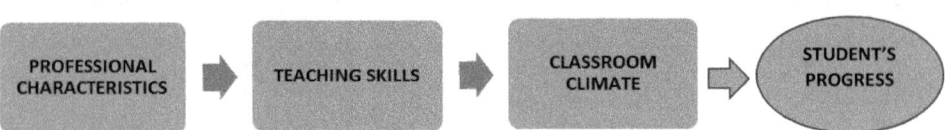

Fig.B.2 (i): Model of teaching effectiveness by McBer (2000)

Although the elements are divergent in nature; each imparts reciprocal actions, so that teachers can understand the unique ways to contribute effectively in teaching. Proficient characteristics and skills equally are input features that provide motivation for students within their classrooms to uphold pupil progress by employing their teaching technique. McBer provided classroom climate as an output measure.

McBer (2000) postulates some of the particular professional characteristics of teachers for making the teaching process effective one equally within and outside the classroom situation, to bring fruitful outcomes. His model shows the following integration of characteristics-

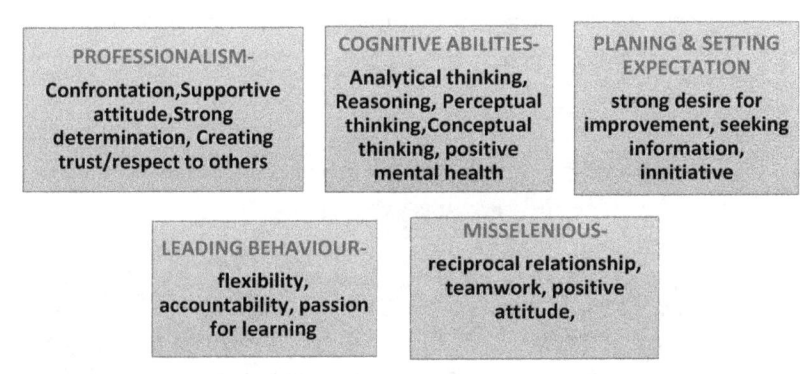

Fig.B.2. (ii): Model of professional characteristics by McBer (2000)

Additionally, McBer (2000) defined skill of teaching as **"diminutive behaviours"** and describe the accessible structure for planning a lesson that teacher can effectively execute during classroom teaching situation. These behaviours were observed with some figure as follows:

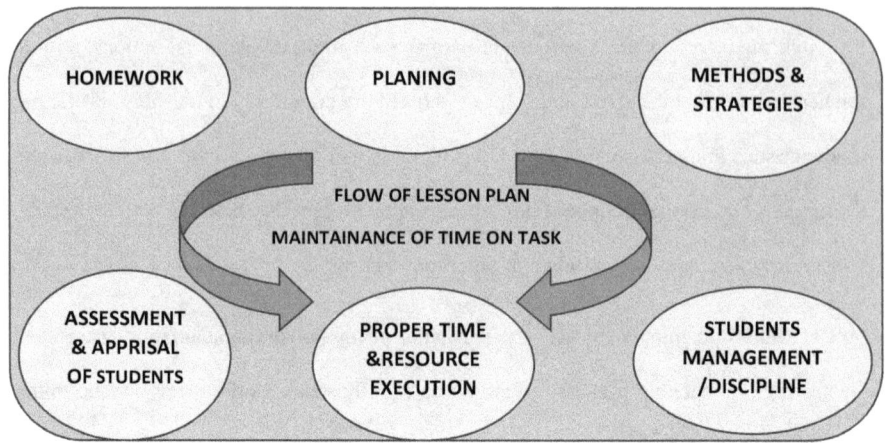

Fig.B.2. (iii): Model of teaching skills by McBer (2000)

Mcber (2000) assumes classroom climate as the **cumulative consciousness** by students about the classroom environment, where those approaches motivate students to learn and also optimize learning opportunities. Classroom climate dimensions represent the following aspects-

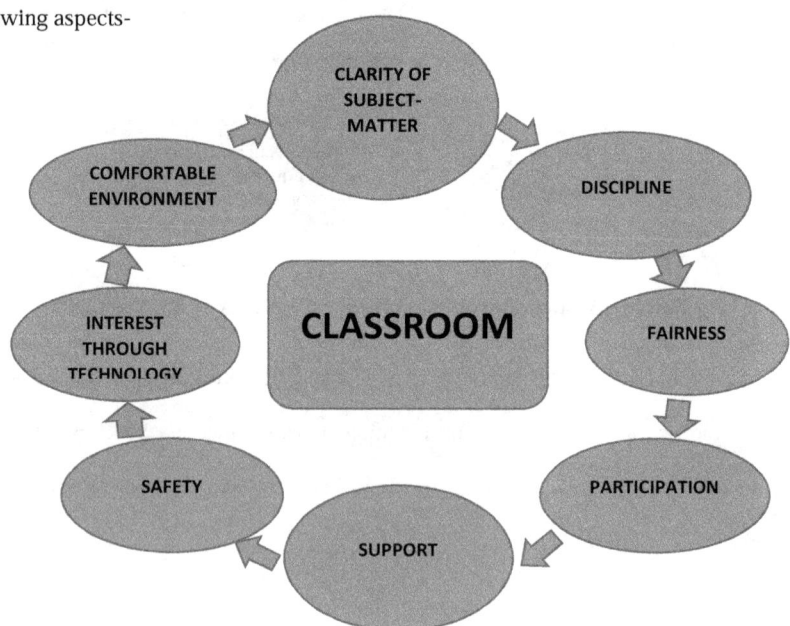

Fig.B.2. (iv): Model of classroom climate by McBer (2000)

McBer (2000) concluded that to create effective teaching-learning ambiance in classroom teachers can make use of their knowledge, behaviours, and skills in a more systematic and productive way.

(ii) Clark &Walsh's (2002) Model of Effective Teacher:

Clark & Walsh's (2002) model emphasizes certain domains that are essential for effective teaching through evaluation and analysis, particularly in subject-matter knowledge, pedagogic knowledge and currently, both in pedagogic and subject-matter knowledge. He also emphasizes teachers' overall professional and personal enhancement which helps them to interface with psycho-physiological, sociological and intellectual development.

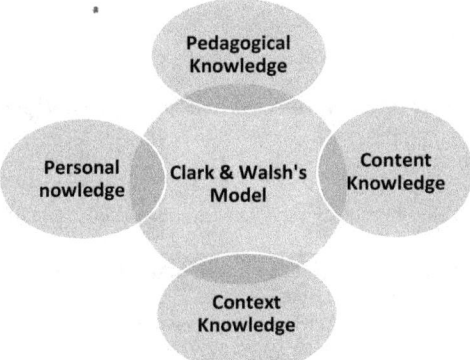

Fig.B.2. (v): Model of effective teacher by Clark & Walsh (2002)

(iii) Teaching Effectiveness Model of Robert Marzano's (2012):

Marzano (2012) has provided a model of teaching effectiveness with some effective strategies and an administrator's tool and support teachers turn out to be more proficient during learning practices. Marzano's causal model emphasizes four domains of professional practice-

AREA-1	AREA-2	AREA-3	AREA-4
Classroom stratagem & behaviour	Planing & arrangement	Deliberating on Teaching	Professsionalism & cooperation

Fig.B.2. (VI): Four domains of professional practice by Robert Marzano's (2012)

Dr. Marzano's (2012) model mainly focussed on developing teachers teaching strategies and students' achievement in the classroom. This model is a unique granular evaluation model that provides feedback regarding teaching strategies to teachers. This innovative framework based design estimates the performance of teacher towards some norms & standard relating to the classroom and also support professional development. This design further illustrates the causal relationship involving strategies of teaching and student achievement.

B.3. Organizational climate as a multifaceted (multidimensional) set up:

One particular construct that has received considerable interest in the domain of teaching performance has been favourable organisational climate to organize and execute required courses of action. Research has suggested organizational climate as a complex and multilevel phenomenon that influences mechanistically the whole structure and system within the framework **(McMurray, Scott, & Pace, 2004)**. Organizational psychologists use the term organizational climate is the perception of employees towards the organization. It has been found that organizational climate affects not only the behaviour and activities of the participants but also their overall wellness and performance as well. Generally, the study of organizational climate found to be related to job satisfaction, personality, behaviour, performance, management style, motivation, structure, technology, etc. In this connection organizational climate will be associated with the psycho-physiological, sociological and pedagogical approaches that contributing overall quality of the educational atmosphere. The term organisational climate is not a concrete discernible concept, it demonstrates the subjective organisational structure that individuals experience and acquire.

The organizational climate is defined as several characteristics concomitant with both external and internal working environment perceived by the staff members (**Mousa & Saudi, 2012)**. These characteristics act as an influential product of the relationship with colleagues, the special needs of the employee, communication style, conflict resolution, and the level of motivation that contributes to the performance of the teachers to achieve the desired result **(Zoubi, 2006)**. Thus, the perceived climate is the outcome of interplay between variables such as employee gratification, collaboration, and efficacy which are important for the organization as well. So, it possibly said that organization performs an authoritative role in the life of human beings. Another undeniable outlook of the perception of organizational climate is the behaviour of teachers **(Raza, 2010)**. An important thing to note is that the climate as perceived by employees of the organization has a determining effect on the behaviour and attitudes of existing members within that ambiance **(Lin & Lee, 2017)**. Apart from these, organizational climate constitutes a metaphor for organizations associated with vulnerable instructional proceedings, perception, beliefs, of these human resource practices. A harmonious organizational climate can promote and provide a healthy influence on employee's productivity of tasks. Generally, Organizational climate aims at a comprehensive and temporal sensation that is subjected to assign effectively with adversity and susceptibility of organizational framework.

Dhivya (2011) evaluates organizational climate as a combination of criterion, ideals, intentions, and some mechanisms that significantly regulate expectancy effort, allegiance, and individual or work unit performance. Therefore, creating a healthy organizational climate with positive interpersonal relationships between staff personnel and the constituents within the institution is considered one of the most important elements. It is also noteworthy that organisational climate is very much pertinent to teaching effectiveness **(Lazaridou & Tsolakidi, 2011)**. In this regard, **(Babu & Kumari, 2013)** identified that high extent of collegiality, humanistic relationship triggering a high level of teaching competency. It is noticeable that satisfying climate undertakes a positive effect upon organizational productivity and hence improve overall educational success. So, the performance of workers is directly related to the perception of organizational climate. The perception of organizational climate also depends on the characteristics of the staff such as level of education, age of the members, area of connectivity and the managerial style.

NCERT's (2005) report presumes two essential and interrelated dimensions i.e. physical and psychological those are strongly associated with organizational climate. Research has suggested organizational climate as the psychosomatic atmosphere that strongly influences the organization in multifarious ways **(Diekhoff, Thompson & Denney, 2006)**. The healthy physical and psychological climate is an important ingredient to not only the successful instructional program but to change overall wellness and provide the preconditions necessary for teaching – learning as well.

Generally speaking, the educational institution today requires energetic and enthusiastic employees with high job involvement attributes. As organisational setting referred to as a place to induce multi-dimensional aspects typically deals with the psycho-physiological environment **(Attkinson & Frechette, 2009)**. In another perspective, it is a deliberately apprehend approach to execute an overall common goal in an attitudinal and value-added manner **(Kaur & Kaur, 2015, p. 56)**. The climate of the organization is the hierarchical unit of a society's social structure and can be interpreted as physical and non-physical conditions realized by the institution **(Maxwell, 2016). Sacher (2010)** illustrates organizational climate as a cognitive framework and prospects shared by the members of the organization.

B.3. (i) Dimensions influencing organizational climate:

In every organization there exist certain aspects that employ an overwhelming impact on the climate. In some organizations construction or arrangements takes a prominent role, whereas to some extent the technical strategies may be a major influential factor of the climate.

Research review has shown different dimension correlated with organisational setting. **James & Jones (1974)** have tried to identify the factors that influencing organizational climate under five heads, contextual setting, structural process, material environment and norms, standards values, etc. Exclusively, fundamental dimensions of any educational climate are relational and the main intensions are to connect people to feel one another cordially.

The Forum Corporation (a global learning and consulting company) **model** describes the perception of organizational climate in two broad concepts i.e. performance and development with six dimensions therein. The performance dimensions dealing with clarity, standards, and commitment. The development dimensions are recognition, responsibility, and teamwork.

➢ **Clarity** refers to the proper responses towards the objectives and policies about their job.

- **Commitment** expresses the extent of employee's continual fidelity to achieve the desired goal. The employee's performance and satisfaction are evaluated through these aspects.
- **Standards** apply the comfortable level of employees in the areas of services, equipment maintenance, and employee training and development and other concessions.
- **Responsibility** is another form of development dimensions of organizational climate. These incorporate personal control over the work, imitativeness, decision-making capacity, sense of autonomy.
- **Recognition** determines the reward of good work, value judgment as a substitute for critique and corporal punishment to get feedback analysis.
- **Teamwork** refers to as the perception of affinity to an organization that is united, one where trustfulness, personal loyalty, and the form of belongingness exist within the organizational surroundings. It exposes the feeling of working together, rather than contrast them.

As a remarkable existence, organizational climate mention as abstract in concept. While making a study of organizational climate, the following aspects that affect the climate in public and private sectors are captured into consideration...

- **Organizational Context:** Organizational context refers to the scope of a parent entity as well as the sub subsistence within the overall organization. It is observable that both human and non-human resources can effectively utilize resources in the existing phenomenon.
- **Organizational Structure:** Structure defined as typical hierarchical arrangement of lines of the institution. It determines the organizational flow like

duty allotment, collaboration and rules & regulations which are coordinated concerning the attainment of organizational goal.

- **Process:** Organizational process assets enable persistent process conduction across the organization and provide acquisition guidance and practices to the organisation. The whole management of the institution carries out certain important processes. These are-

1. Decision-making: This process involves problem-solving skills, determining resource allocations, fund distribution and also transform work.

2. Training: It encompasses predefined and some systematic modification of behaviour through some educational events, seminars, instruction to achieve knowledge, skill, and competency.

3. Communication: It mainly addresses the interchange of information, intentions, and outlook inside and outside the organisation. Communication certainly denotes the network of interdependent relationships with the explicit flow of information.

4. Motivation: It is a psychological driving force of stimulating workers to accomplish determined objectives.

5. Organizational innovativeness and Changes: Organizational change concerning the process of developing organizational policies, procedures, responsibilities, technologies, culture, as well as the consequences of such transition on organization.

- **Physical Environment:** Physical Environment has been observed as an employee's work atmosphere, number of branch offices and situation of head office, size and location of the building, etc. which have an essential effect on inculcation of a healthy attitude towards the working place.

➢ **System Values and Norms**: These elements consisting of faith, optimism, and norms for manifesting the responses of the individual as an active member of the institution. The legitimacy of behaviour, abstract sentiments or ideals, impartiality is broadly considered to be an expecting factor in itself.

➢ **Relationship between superiors and subordinates:** The relationship between co-workers represents a supreme alliance between the employee and the organizational authority. If the employees are not satisfied then the teaching-learning endeavour will be hindered. Therefore, participative and effective communication must consider the proper functioning of the organisational climate.

B.3. (ii) Models comprising parameters of organizational climate:

Patterson et al. (2005) postulate a value framework comprising four quarters to originate and justify a multiform procedure of organizational climate. These models comprehending aligning position along with some dimensional overview **(Imran, et al., 2010).**

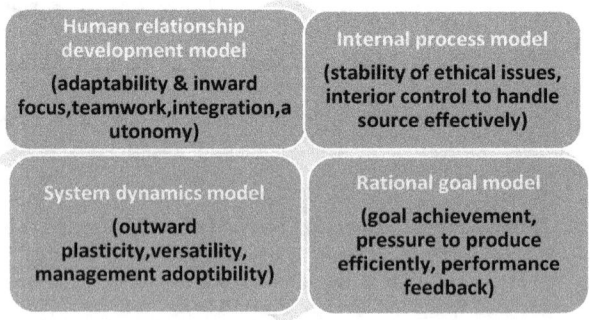

Fig.B.3. (i): Organizational climate dimensions by Patterson et al. (2005)

Furthermore, organisational climate denotes structural dimensions which closely related to those inherent objective characteristics.

a) Structural **D**imension
b) **I**nterpersonal **D**imension
c) **I**ndividual **D**imension

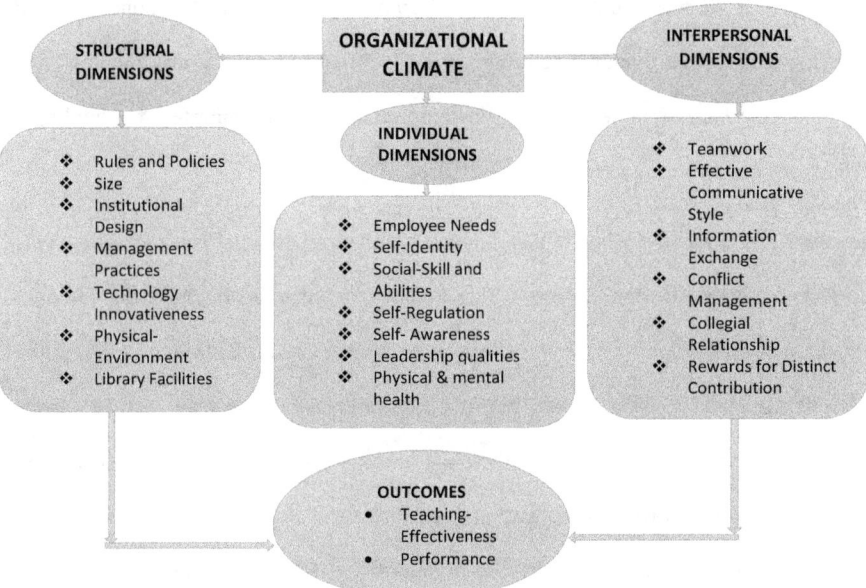

Fig.B.3. (ii): Educational climate substructure

In fact, the organizational climate will combine these three dimensions in a manner inseparable from each other. Conclusively, from the above stating phenomenon the predictable organisational climate model which will exemplify the whole educational climate substructure can be depicted as shown above.

These two theories and models clearly point to the importance of an effective organizational setting in the path of overall workers' development. According to this model, the climate is formed by objective aspects of the organizational structure. Undoubtedly, organizational climate is a crucial input in maintaining and raising the educational standard. Indeed, the subjective component of the study of organizational climate is critical, while the employee tends to respond emotionally to discern environmental settings. Therefore, the perception of organizational climate can be recognised as derives inputs from the environmental factors, in that point it is not isolation from the surrounding environment of the organization. For making classroom as effective centres for the teaching –learning situation, it is important for holding a productive and skilful workforce.

Research reviews have shown that mental health promotion efforts are effectively correlated with a safe, participatory and responsive organizational climate that provides the optimal foundation for learning **(Berkowitz & Bier, 2006; Catalano et. al., 2002; Greenberg et. al., 2003)**. Perception of organizational climate also focused on the outcomes of employee's mental health which are associated with several factors. These include: 1) work attitudes, 2) motivation 3) performance, etc. **(Parker et al., 2003)**. So, mental health continues to be crucial in organisational setting. It might have an effect directly or indirectly and significantly or insignificantly on the mental health of workers too.

Also, information technology is received a considerable amount of professional attention in the teaching-learning condition, as the development of technology could bring changes at large. ICT has come out as exclusively undeniable aspects of the human being. It is considered as a new way of illustrating, imparting and was a copy with current information **(Gupta, 2015)**. Even in college, the use of the internet has increased at a fluster rate; so, the positive attitude of teachers towards the implementation of ICT is crucial. Presently, educational institutions are also remoulding themselves into smart skyrocketing with the help of ICT exertion. That is the reason; ICT has stood out as a researchable topic in teaching-learning discourse. In this present study, mental health and attitude towards ICT are discussed in the following paragraphs in detail.

B.4. Mental health as a challenge in the workplace:

Mental health is one of the major focuses of psychology and other social science professionals. The main purpose of studying the concept of mental health is to improve the psychological well-being of an individual. It is the way that individuals act, think and feel. In this regard, the term 'mental health' is in some cases used to mean a complete absence of a mental issue. Especially, the mental state of the people is diagnosed as one of the enormous mishaps of the modernised, expeditious world. Mental wellness is a term used comprehensively, whereby the individual has to adjust according to the stipulation and convenience of life. The indication 'Mental Health' comprises two phases- The term 'Mental' normally implicit the existence that is entirely related to the epistemic performing of a person along with the established equilibrium relationship of socio-cultural context. Similarly, the phrase 'Health' denotes individuals both intra-psychic and inter-psychic balance and also certain functioning relating to social and cultural matters **(Kaur, 2007)**. So, mental health stands as indicative of good physical and psycho-social health or well-being. Accordingly, the mental health concept corresponding to the wholesomeness of mind, physique, organs and their functioning. **Singh (2004)** postulates mental health as a state of psychical well-being, or absenteeism of mental illness according to the laymen's perspective. It might incorporate life fulfilment, a feeling of control, having reason throughout everyday life, a feeling of having a place and positive associations with others **(Mathers & Loncar, 2005).** Mental health has customarily been characterized as the nonattendance of psychopathology.

According to World Health Organization (WHO, 2001) reports mental health includes the combination of indigenous happiness, perceivable self-adequacy, self-reliance, capability, and intra-generational dependency, self-realization of one's cognitive and psychological perspective with others. **Galgotra (2013)** signifies that mentally healthy people manifest equitable behaviour and can hold the multifarious realities of life, courageously. It is also significant that they can live their existing lifestyle adequately and effectively with another living organism of society.

According to **Chauhan (2011)** *"mental health is a situation of psychological maturity. It is a condition of personal and social performance with a maximum of effectiveness"*. In fact, salutary mental health is identified by the means of harmonious functioning of maximum personalized productiveness, successful outcomes, pleasure and supremacy of well-formed functioning as a whole. It is the challenge to maintain beneficial mental health; as it tends to continue continuous adaptation of inherent delightfulness as well as societal wellness and improvement simultaneously. So, to sustain healthy mental health, it continues as a dynamic challenging process. When a person has firm intentions to cope up with day-to-day stress and strains, then they can strive to achieve a balance aspiration of life. So, it is an important aspect to permit realistic maintenance of an optimistic overview to stick in the process of well-being.

In contemporary society, the life of human being is presenting very composite and paradoxical gradually. Further, the individual in the present time is not merely the absence of mental illness. The mental health of a person carries diversified changes in life, irrespective of hereditary causes, the stressors relating to the environment or the occurrence of material changes during their life expectancy **(Holmes, 2001)**. **Bhatia (1982)** considers mental health as the ability to face and accept the realities of life with a higher level of desires, ambitions, and ideals in one's daily living. It is undeniable fact that due to fast-paced moving social forces, mental health adjustment also changing by various factors. So, it is necessary for an individual to maintain a better condition of psychological and biological efficiency to carry out healthy contribution. A short while ago, inclusively mental health has surfaced as a close causal association with learning. For any type of education, sound mental health is the first condition. As we concern that teacher predominantly play a significant position to possess effective learning conditions in the classroom. **Singh (1992)** concluded that *"a teacher with poor mental health not only tends to incapacitate himself for the performance of his multifarious duties in the organization but also creates difficulties and problems for his students"* **(Bappan, 2018)**. So, sound mental health is an unavoidable predisposition for both teachers and students. In this support, sound mental health is the first priority to allow the function of harmonious co-ordination, full expressions of subject-matter and so on.

In recent years, a psychotherapist in conjunction with education professionals has arrived to create awareness in the field of mental health. However, in India, comparatively minimal works have been carried out. In the current day, mental health is certified as a prominent exposure of one's complete health status which may regard as a primary factor. Just as it ensues necessary for everyone to maintain good physical health and it is needy to stand for every human being towards the importance of achieving equity in sound positive health worldwide. In the broader perspective, mental health has been identified as the extent of research that puts a preference in upgrading the totality of experiences for attaining overall well-being.

B.4. (i) Dimensions of mental health:

Good physiological health can improve the quality of life. Adequate mental balancing and durability is a directing factor in a person's habitual life. In the recent past, scholars have contended for integrated models of mental health, which involve both the truancy of major psychopathic symptoms and the companionship with good thoughts, loving concern and positive behavioural patterns **(Keyes, et.al 2010).** The aspects of a mentally healthy person denote the stability of mind in the midst of adverse circumstances. In this study, the perspective of mental health connotes to identify the teachers' health condition for promoting effective teaching circumstances.

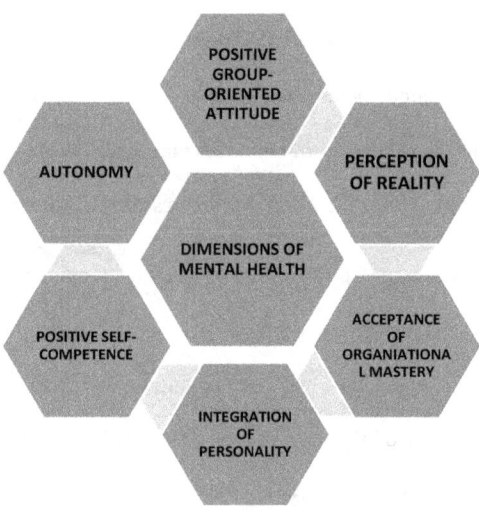

Fig.B.4. (i): Dimensions of mental health

Dimensions of mental health are as follows:

- **Positive group-oriented attitude:** It is combined with the collaborative ability with positive vibes towards the implementation of teaching strategies.
- **Perception of reality:** It is associated with the perception free from misrepresentation, the dearth of excessive imagination and an extensive outlook towards reality.
- **Acceptance of organizational mastery:** It includes the ability to work efficiently to meet the situational requirements, and also to take whole responsibilities and capacity for adaptation.
- **Integration of personality:** It implies the integration of both the individual and collective unconscious of the personality. Personality integration indicates all psycho-physical forces such as psychological needs, interests, attitude, aptitude, emotions, and morphology, etc.
- **Positive self-competence:** These aspects inculcate the feeling of worthiness, attainment of one's potentialities, and also the interrelationship between self-perception of personal worth and efficacy.
- **Autonomy:** It signifies the self-dependence quality rather than interdependence. This aspect includes the stability of internal standards, dependence for own development to achieve self-potentialities.

Hence, mental health conditions completely based on the well-adjustment capacity of an individual with a maximum of effectiveness, the capacity of confronting and obtaining the actualities of life. Especially, in the educational sector, the teacher must be the custodian of sound mental health. But, sometimes it may difficult to remain with consistency. In this situation, teachers have to face a constant challenge to stick in being professionally competent, skilled, healthy position to contribute to teaching. This can be exacting for some teachers, particularly when they are facing mental health problems.

B.4. (ii) Mental health scenario of teachers:

In the present day, the overall sketch of teachers depicts that the maximum number of them are bound to be contrived by a particular amount of stressors. Research has observed that teacher grief is normally related to lack of government support, the persistent need for the new curriculum, family and social environment, insufficient educational funds, work overload, etc. **(Travers & Cooper 1996; Dewan 2012)**. In India, the mental health position of teachers has been evaluated by different investigators and produced inconsistent outcomes **(Kaur, 2011; Dewan, 2012; Lath, 2012; Galgotra, 2013; Patel, 2013)**. So, currently, it is a consequential issue to get concern about mental health complications. The report of the **World Health Organization (2000-2001)** has declared that 20-25% of the world population is strained by mental related problems which consider as inevitable during their life.

Canadian Teachers Federation (2014) reported that 93% of teachers are fronting many complexities in leading work-life balance and 90% experienced imbalanced class composition due to workload stress **(Bennett, 2014).** Quebec is the capital city of the Canadian province, in a research finding, shows that 12 to 20% of teachers are suffered intellectual problems weekly basis **(Fernet, Guay, Senecal, & Austin, 2012)**. The reports support the deteriorating mental health status of educators. The recent research **(From April 2017 to March 2018)** indicates that teachers seeking mental health support increased gradually and the rate is distinct as 35% in the past 12 months. According to the 2017 health survey report of the UK, education professionals have faced job-related stressed most of the time in the past few weeks **(Stanley, 2018).**

Another relation to Britain's teachers' survey shows that over and above half a portion of them are pinpointed with mental health abnormalities. Every eight (8) in ten (10) respondents (81%) teachers express that poor mental health leads to a negative effect on maintaining quality relationships with students. The crucial reason for that is workload pressure and increasing financial strain given among the staff members **(Bulman, 2018)**. American Federation of Teachers survey clearly pointed out that a greater proportion of American teachers undergo work-related strain. In particular, 61% of teachers say that they always or often stressed out their work and 58% of teachers narrate their physiological condition is not satisfactory. Over half of respondents agree that they don't consider energetic and enthusiasm in teaching as before **(Mahnken, 2017)**.

The WHO has concluded that anxiety and depression will be intended as the immense exhaustion to the community as well as society by 2020 which may affect the whole physical and intellectual prosperity. Indeed, professional exhaustion has significantly assigned to an unnecessary destructive evacuation from the profession **(Smithers & Robinson, 2003)**. Conceivably in reaction, the UK and the rest of Europe revived some scheme agenda to prevent mental compliant and for better promotion of health positions**(Europe, 2008; European Union High-level Conference, 2008)**.Yet, exceeding 40% of countries risen up with mental health policy, beyond 90% of adolescents and children have no strategic mental health, and in case of further 30% have no identified mental health programs (World Health Organization, The World Health Report 2001).For all such conditions, there is an increasing demand for better enhancement of physical, psychological and overall health concerns among teachers.

Indian perspective: A study conducted in **NIMHANS**, Bangalore (2010) reported that the population ranged from 9.5 to 102 per 1000 experienced mental and behavioural disorders **(Math & Srinivasaraju, 2010)**. Another report of **WHO (2018)**, conducted for the NCMH (National Care Of Medical Health), exhibits that almost 6.5 % of the Indian population bears the severe form of mental disorder in both the rural-urban arena. It also found that in India & China both men and women are confronted with anxiety and pessimism problems among the age group of 20-69 years **(Mental Health in the Workplace, 2017)**. Experts inculcate that mental illness arises because of unhappiness; depression comprises one in every four people **(WHO, 2017)**.

In turn, the effectiveness is very much dependent on the psychological wellbeing of the teachers **(Kaur, 2015)**. Another important aspect **(Panda & Patra, 2017)** inculcated that overall mental health can affect the teacher's perception of organizational climate. Additionally, the study indicated that teachers also appeared to benefit from using ICTs for their mental health recovery. Receiving support through ICTs appears to increase their mental condition by reducing the feeling of stigma **(Fulford et al., 2016)**.

B.5. ICT and teacher attitude:

In the novel edge of eternity, information and communication technology (ICT) has brought new possibilities nearly in all emerging regions. As are evolutionary tool, the technology-related scheme helps in developing teaching procedures in the illumination of the betterment of educational process around the sphere **(Kahveci, Sahin & Genc, 2011)**. Al-Qahtani & Higgins, (2013) remarked the extension of technology has brought a wide range of educational institutions one step closer with an aspiration of improving the teaching and learning environment. Several theoreticians prolonged that teachers' attitudinal change has a sturdy influence on technology integration in educational settings **(Albirini, 2006; Huang & Liaw, 2005; Mahajan 2016)**. Therefore, to nourish with the moving world brought by technology, teachers need to furnish and acquaint themselves to be associated with the collaborative transformation **(Cuban, 2001; Kozma, McGhee, Quellmalz & Zalles, 2004; Philip, Oluwagbemi,& Oluwaranti, 2010; Voogt 2010).**

Freeman (1968) defines attitude as *"A dispositional readiness to respond to certain situations, persons or objects in a consistent manner which has been learned and has become one's typical mode or response."*

Thurstone (1959) defines attitude as *"the degree of the positive or negative effect associated with some psychological objects."*

These definitions show that an attitude is a preparation or readiness for the response. It is incipient rather than overt and consummator. Attitude has great importance in learning practices. It is one of the important aspects of developing attitudes in the aspects and process of school subjects. It has well-articulated that ICT moves as the thresholdfor enhancing the propagation of information as it helps teachers to be modernized. In the prevailing situation, ICT represents a new approach to meet various challenges in the system of education and has become a nucleus of the profession. But, in the midst of educational and scientific development teachers' attitudes are regarded as the key innovation representatives. That is why the teachers' role in the 21st century is deflecting to an essential assignment as a portrayal frontier for applying technological innovations in teaching processes. Research also supported the great extent of technology use in teaching practices depends largely on the right attitude to be cultivated for teachers towards ICTs **(Albirini, 2006; Baylor & Ritchie, 2002)**.

Similarly, **Kersaint et al. (2003)** exhibit that teachers with an affirmative change in attitude towards technology, have experienced more comfort during the time of using it. Attitude towards ICT is the inclination of acceptance or rejection of a tool for learning with the choice of preferentially positive and negative responses. Teachers' positive attitudes towards the use of ICT are inclined by factors such as training **(Tsitouridou & Vryzas, 2003)**, awareness about technology implemented devices **(Mukti, 2000)**, anxiety related to technology **(Yildirim, 2000)** and know-how to use technological devices in teaching-learning process **(Kumar & Kumar, 2003)**. **Becker et al. (1999) and G**obbo **& Girardi (2001)** indicated that there is a positive association between technology training and teachers' attitudes. Studies inculcated that optimistic outlook brings about stimulation, exclusiveness, productiveness of the teacher, and also implement for new teaching techniques **(Albirini, 2004)**. As the infusion of technology in pedagogical approaches tends to motivate the learners, foster inquiry, exploration, transform the present knowledge by using authentic and also active learning paradigm. Therefore, there is the necessity for proper utilization of ICT in parallel with mastery over technological skills. Hence, many studies **(Sang, Valcke, Van Braak, & Tondeur, 2010)** have reported that the attitude related to computer and usability of technology in pedagogical practices is considered as a crucial point.

According to the **UNESCO report (2002)** *"ICT is a scientific, technological and engineering discipline and management technique used in handling information, its application and association with social, economic and cultural matters."* While there are many definitions of ICT it can be broadly defined as *"technologies which are facilitated by electronic means, the acquisition, storage, processing, transmission, and disseminating of information in all forms including voice, text, data, graphics, and* *video"* (**Michiels & Van Crowder, 2001**). This definition mainly focuses on the importance of the intersection of information technology, information content, and telecommunications in enabling new forms of knowledge production and interactivity. **Ndongfack (2015)** considered ICT as pillars upon quality education which can reflect the reality to bring the world together even from most remote and disadvantaged communities.

When focusing on the inclusion of ICT to carry on the achievement of educational purposes, it is noticed that required awareness not yet fully integrated especially in developing and underdeveloped countries. The Information and Communication Technology (ICT) in the curriculum can provide a broad perspective on the usability and applicability of various technologies, and also the effect of ICT on society.

B.5. (i) ICT as a Changing Agent in Higher Education:

The most striking metamorphosis in the area of higher education is the integration of ICT in education. It is important to note that managing ICT to combine the quality of education has influenced diverse scenarios across different colleges **(Neeru, 2009)**. Primarily, colleges are an important sector of the higher education system through which the development of ICT and other digital systems can be brought to fulfilment. In the higher education system in India, basically in the college level, the innovative and transformational impact of technology on teaching-learning strategies acts as a **"knowledge superpower"**. The innovative use of ICT can strengthen the whole education scenario by lessening the challenges of access, equity, and quality.

The system of higher education has expanded in an exponential manner to reach the necessity of value education for all due to swift advancements in ICT. A study reported by the International Institute for Communication and Development (IICD) that 80% of educators perceived more alertness and empowered by their vulnerability to ICT in education, and 60% felt that that the entire educational processes were directly and positively affected by the use of ICT **(Vijayalaxmi,2016)**. The speedy development of Information and Communication Technology (ICT) especially the internet is one of the key fascinating phenomena specifying the digital era **(Sarkar, 2012)**. Supporting this point **Yusuf, (2005)** reported that the field of higher education has been overblown by ICTs which have certainly touched teaching, learning and research activities. ICT act as a driving force and enabling the productive processes toward a knowledge-based universal economy. It allows higher education providers to accommodate the specific needs of students according to their place, mode terms, time of study and to oblige the facility to different new target groups both locally and globally.

- ➤ **Upgrade Educational Process**: ICT can mold the teaching-learning process more effective and facilitate learning with the help of using different audio-visual aids in the classroom.
- ➤ **Vast Variety of Study Material**: Use of ICT facilities for students to access a variety of course materials on a specific topic using the internet from anyplace at any moment.
- ➤ **Accommodate with Research Activities**: ICT tools have also been extensively applied for the researcher to get access to thousands of online journals, articles, e-Books, and publications, etc.
- ➤ **ICT in Remedial Courses**: A remedial teaching class is one that is meant to improve learning skills or to rectify a particular problem faced by a student. Here, in remedial teaching, the course structure is designed by instructional

material for students which will be accessible in the website with the help of ICT.

- **ICT as an Assessment Technique**: The use of ICT can help teachers by storing and recording information to know about the student's development and understanding of new material. Providing feedback to students is a very important aspect.
- **Virtual Lab**: ICT provides flexibility to a learner to get acquainted with online laboratory sessions and can take different types of objectives, specimens, models; equipment's to do their practical freely at any moment.
- **Development of instructional material**: ICT is devised for the purpose of the learning process as a manifold set of technological tools and materials used to transmit, create, circulate, accumulate and manage information.
- **Web-blogs and Wikipedia**: A weblog is created for educational purposes for sharing information and tips among colleagues, providing information for students. Wikipedia, an online encyclopaedia, which provides collaborative working on a group project as users can edit content.
- **Wireless classroom microphones**: This is another form of devices through which the students can able to hear clearly from teachers without disturbances.
- **Digital video-on-demand**: Digital video eradicates the need for in-classroom hardware and permits both the teachers and students to retrieve the material immediately.
- **Online media**: Streamed video websites can be utilized to enhance a classroom lesson.

> **Online study tools**: Tools that motivate students by assembling the subject-matter more fun or individualized for the student.

Additionally, it can be realized that technology may accomplish the possible benefits in the educational process. In order to provide this awareness, teachers should be well acquainted with the integration of technology from the grass-root level. Any reflective access to the content and learning resources through ICT is a network in classrooms. The entrance of ICT into different fields of activities and its daily-increase development in the current century is a valuable chance for specialists and involved people in education.

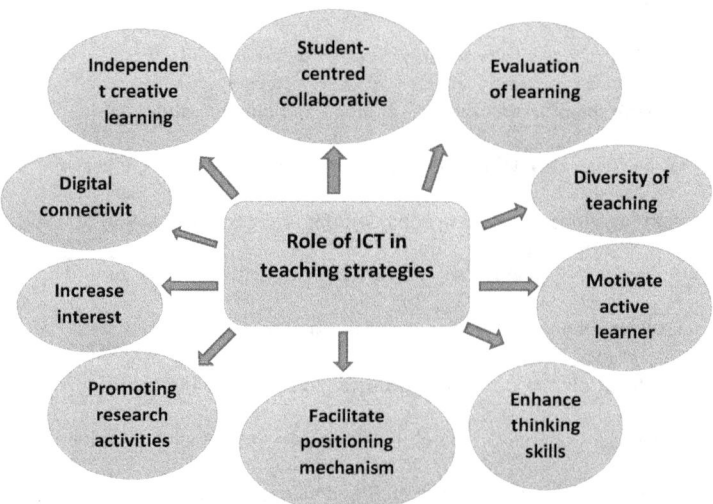

Fig.B.5. (i): Model for Improving teaching and learning through ICT

B.5. (ii) Models of ICT: (Ghosh & Guha, 2016).

(a) TPACK Model (Technological Pedagogical Content Knowledge):

Pedagogic Use of ICT in a Classroom:

Shulman (1986) asserts that teachers must have firm knowledge about the content areas of their discipline. He stated that the lack of content knowledge in teaching strategies may lead to ineffective teaching approaches and classroom management. So, this model emphasizes the important connection of pedagogic and content knowledge for teaching in the classroom environment.

Shulman´s PCK model was originated by **Mishra and Koehler (2006)** by adding the installation of technology with the content and pedagogical knowledge to constitute effective learning processes. They strongly accepted that **TPACK** is a useful model that tends to negotiate the reciprocity of technology, pedagogy, and content for making learning more systematic and effective and more enchanting. Generally, this technological innovative model is equipped as an open-ended learning situation. **Mishra & Koelher (2006)** insisted that when teachers are furnished with adequate technological knowledge with content and pedagogy, then effective teaching with ICT can be inculcated.

Furthermore, many studies have observed the relationship between technology and teacher-related pedagogical beliefs. **Voogt, Fisser, Pareja Roblin, Tondeur, & Van Braak (2013)** state the influence of ICT to foster the knowledge of effective teaching with active involvement in incorporated courses. **Agyei & Voogt, (2012)** also encompasses that the collaborative design of TPACK improves communication style and knowledge relating to relevant information. This study also inculcated the efficiency of teachers who use computers in the classroom are more innovative than others. **Voogt (2010)** included that the prevalence of ICT usage has positively correlated with pedagogical learning outcomes. **Khan (2002)** analyzed varieties of useful on-line learning environments which has presented a framework for e-learning as well. He believes that a regular understanding of ICT application may provide better effectiveness in learning. **Khan** said that for a reflective learning environment it is necessary for suitable changes in the field of ICT application. He also emphasizes the measurement of self-evaluation and also the ethical dimensions for effective technological progress.

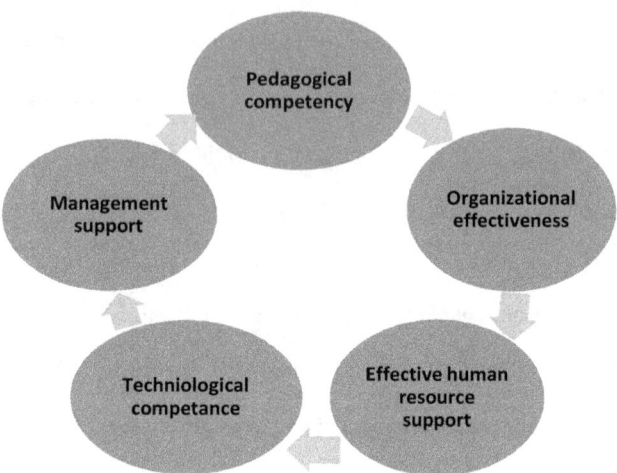

Fig.B.5. (ii): Models of ICT framework in teaching

(b) Unified Theory of Acceptance and Use of Technology (TUAUT): (Venkatesh et al., 2003) represents this model as the individual's intention to accept the ICT in higher institutions. The basic concepts of user acceptance models are associated with three useful links i.e. being familiar with ICT integration; next, transformation and finally, expansion of information technology to the educational endeavor.

This three main aspects of ICT are depicted as-

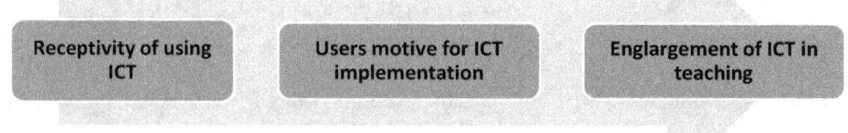

Fig.B.5. (iii): Aspects of ICT

The above figure illustrates the effect of the TUAUT model to accept the use of new technology. It means that the reaction of teachers towards ICT will determine their acceptance and also current educational use. Model TUAUT contains five direct determinants concerning their acceptance and use of technology. These are...

a) The execution expectancy to achieve job performance.

b) The effort anticipation which is associated with the use of ICT.

c) The social influence that considers a person's perception of using new technology.

d) The organizational and technical infrastructure to facilitate the use of technological systems.

e) The behavioral intention of users to accept ICT.

The above model describes all aspects which contribute to ICT implementation in the learning procedure. The models have explained ICT integration on diverse perspectives, which are suitable in this study. But the present study is befitted with **Khan, (2003)** technology framework, so the main focus will be only on it.

B.5. (iii) Notable initiatives for implementing ICT in Indian education landscape:

Recognizing the significance of the educational program, the government has accepted several estimates to facilitate the acquisition of ICT equipment. The central government, as well as the state government, has implemented several indigenous as well as nation-specific schemes related to ICT in higher education. Indian higher education is disseminated with discrete councils responsible for the regulation of different institutions. The Government of India has strongly taken ICT initiatives and has laid down a National ICT policy, which is reflected and implemented through various Government Departments and Ministries. It is being implemented through various activities of the **N**ational **I**nformatics Center (**NIC**) and encouragements from University Grants Commission (**UGC**), **A**ll **I**ndia Council of Technical Education (**AICTE**) and **D**epartment of Science & Technology (**DST**) throughout the country. National **A**ssociation of Services and Software Companies (**NASSCOM**) have also played a pivotal role in the formulation of these policies **(Sharma &Singh 2010).** The main tertiary level governing body is the University Grants Commission through which healthy coordination between the central and the state can be enforced.

1) **The National Mission on Education:** It has anticipated as a centrally funded scheme to grip the power of ICT. The scheme plan to focus on certain appropriate pedagogical approaches such as….

   - Providing e-learning & **O**n-line accessibility of teachers to mentor the learners.
   - Performance of different experiments through virtual laboratories including new web-based resources, video-lectures, self-evaluation, and animated demonstrations, etc.
   - Usages of accessible **E**ducational **S**atellite (**EduSAT**) and direct to home (**DTH**) platforms. (**IT & ICT**, http://www.sakshat.ac.in)
   - SAKSHAT portal is an effort of **NMEICT** towards creating an open house for knowledge.
   - **A**nother distinct initiative provided by MHRD is E-PG Pathsala through ICT (NME-ICT). It is solitary storage of online-resources comprising, NCERT textbooks and other learning resources together with textbooks, audio, video, periodicals, and various form of print and non-print materials.

2) The Ministry for **Human Resource Development (MHRD)** has validated the initiative, which will now be executed in a phased manner **(Times News Network, April 22, 2007)**. MHRD grasped a spring towards the transformation of the education sector with the phrase of "Education for All &Quality Education" with some guided policies. Some of the notable examples are-

- The **Swayam Prabha** a web portal has been designed as the **DTH** program for educational excellence. It is completely digital with high quality educational programs on a 24X7 basis. So, in the higher education domain; this portal has covered multidisciplinary course contents in a detailed manner **(Press Information Bureau, 2016)**.

- **Global Initiative** of **Academic Network (GIAN)**: Indian Govt. was approved this new scheme to boost the quality of higher education on November 0, 2015 **[India Today, 2015]**.

- **Impacting Research Innovation and Technology (IMPRINT)**: It is a unique initiative in India to boost original scientific and technological research in the country. It is a joint commencement of the Indian Institutes of Technology (IITs) and the Indian Institute of Science (IISc).

- **National Institutional Ranking Framework (NIRF)**: This framework was supported by the MHRD and launched by the Honorable Minister of Human Resource Development on 29th September 2015.

- **Digital ISBN:** This portal has launched by The Hon'ble Human Resource Development minister on 7th April 2016. ISBN Portal is a part of the e-governance initiative for streamlining the process of registration, overcome delayed response, problems like loss of documents, etc.

- ➢ **Vittiya Saksharata Abhiyan (VISAKA)**: The ministry of HRD launched VISAKA on 1st December 2016. It is a transformational shift through which students can give consistent feedback and instructions related to course material.

- ➢ **National Programme on Technology Enhanced Learning (NPTEL):** This project was initiated from 2003 financed by MHRD, Govt. of India. NPTEL provides E-learning resources through online Web and Video courses of various streams.

3) **All India Council for Technical Education (AICTE):** SWAYAM, an indigenous an online Massive Open Online Courses (MOOCS) platform is being developed by AICTE with support from MHRD. In the nutshell, this IT platform transformed the educational process by providing the best quality course material covering all the subject- matter with free of cost, especially for college and university level. The initiative is also supported through "Pradhan Mantri Kaushal Vikas Yojana" **(AICTE, 2019).**

4) **University Grants Commission (UGC):** UGC instigate remarkable initiatives to use **INFONET** and CEC (Consortium for Educational Communication) services in various universities and colleges to support online-content, courses and also online learning systems. Information and Library Network (INFLIBNET) Centre is an Autonomous Inter-University Centre (IUC) of University Grants Commission (UGC) involved sharing of library and information resources and services among Academic and Research Institutions

(Neeru, 2009). For instance, Gyan Darshan was launched in 2000 to telecast educational programs for university students and adults. Also, under the UGC, countrywide e-content classroom learning initiatives are stated as encouraging creation for the improved stage of educational processes in colleges and universities. The Rashtriya Uchchatar Shiksha Abhiyan (RUSA) launched in 2013, to provide funding, reforms in academic and adequate availability of equity in higher educational institutions.

To achieve this expanding demand, Indian educational institutions have been expeditious to accept Information and Communications Technology (ICT), taking the technology-based teaching-learning strategies at universities and colleges to a higher level, as observed by Priyanka Sharma of Elets News Network (**ENN**).

Although the quick advancement regarding ICT use greatly affects all domains of occupational settings; the educators' review mainly exhibits the impact of ICT on the study environment. However, it enables the recognition and prioritization of research requirements, which are very much influential intrans forming towards a solid knowledge base on the association between ICT use and mental health.

Section C: Conceptualization of the study

C.1. Statement of the problem:

In a country like India, most of the time education becomes a benchmark for professional up- gradation, career advancement, and status in society, etc. People of modern times, especially in India, give more importance to academics. Most importantly quality education is always a debatable topic. Research has already suggested that to make a quality-based education system, teachers should be well qualified, fully professional, knowledgeable, skilled and effective. From age-old practices, it boils down to three things which are most important for a healthy classroom environment and these are teachers' competencies, healthy organisational settings, and mental health consequences. So, for making education fruitful, there is always a need for the proper combination of these aforementioned factors. Also, it is noteworthy that good or congenial climate is always regarded as the secret behind the success of any institution which can also enhance the effectiveness of educators. Again, in today's competitive world maintaining a healthy body and mind also treat as a threatening issue which always reflects in professional work.

21st century has scaled many heights in science and technology, and new technological innovations have touched almost every sector including education. Our need for education is diversified and extensive, as new India requires more individuals who are equipped with specific technical skills. A mentally sound person with effective knowledge can contribute efficiently to teaching new generations with modern technological innovations. Ultimately, a general theme can be made that efficiency and technology go hand in hand and in combination they can enhance the personal and academic environment in a good teaching endeavour. Therefore, in this study, an attempt has been made to find out and analyse if there exists any relationship between teaching effectiveness with three inter-related variables viz. Organisational climate, mental health and attitude towards ICT of college teachers based on their gender, locality, and duration of experience, etc. That eventually inspired the investigator to pursue the study under the following heading:

Teaching Effectiveness of College Teachers in Relation to Organisational Climate, Mental Health and Attitude towards ICT.

C.2.Research Questions:

Thus, the present research attempts to seek answers to the following research questions:
1. Is there any relationship that exists between teaching effectiveness, organisational climate, mental health and attitude towards ICT?
2. **Do** teaching effectiveness, organisational climate, mental health and attitude towards ICT differ with gender, locality, and duration of experience?

C.3.Research Objectives:
- To find out and compare the teaching effectiveness of male and female college teachers.
- To find out and compare the level of teaching effectiveness of rural and urban college teachers.
- To find out and compare the level of teaching effectiveness based on the duration of experience (1-10, 11-20, and above 21years).
- To find out and compare the perception of organizational climate of male and female college teachers.
- To find out and compare the perception of organizational climate of rural and urban college teachers.
- To find out and compare the perception of organizational climate of college teachers based on length of experience (1-10, 11-20, and above21 years).
- To find out and compare the mental health of male and female college teachers.
- To find out and compare the mental health of rural and urban college teachers.
- To find out and compare the mental health of college teachers based on the duration of experience (1-10, 11-20, and above21years).

- To find out and compare the attitude towards ICT of male and female college teachers.
- To find out and compare the attitude towards ICT of rural and urban college teachers.
- To find out and compare the attitude towards ICT of college teachers based on the duration of experience (1-10, 11-20, and above 21years).
- To find out whether there is any relationship between the teaching effectiveness and the perception of organizational climate of college teachers.
- To investigate the correlation between teaching effectiveness and mental health of the college teachers.
- To investigate the relationship between the teaching effectiveness of college teachers and their attitude towards ICT.
- To study the relationship between the perception of organizational climate and mental health of college teachers.
- To find out whether there is any relationship between the perception of organizational climate and attitude towards ICT of college teachers.
- To find out the correlation between mental health and attitude towards ICT among college teachers.

C.4. Hypotheses of the Study:

Taking into account the literature available and based on the independent variables of the study, some null hypothesis is formulated for empirical verifications. To test the significance of difference, the null hypothesis is a useful technique. Because it is better to think no differences exist between the two variables until it is proved scientifically. In the present study, the researcher wants to check if there is any differences exist, so the researcher decided to formulate the null hypothesis. The following are the null hypothesis formulated to test the tenability of the hypothesis.

(Ho1) There will be no significant difference in teaching effectiveness of male and female college teachers.

(Ho2) There will be no significant difference in the locality (rural/urban) on teaching effectiveness of college teachers.

(Ho3) There will be no significant difference in duration of experience on teaching effectiveness of college teachers.

(Ho4) There will be no significant difference in the perception of organizational climate of male and female college teachers.

(Ho5) There will be no significant difference in the perception of organizational climate of rural and urban college teachers.

(Ho6) There will be no significant difference in the perception of organizational climate of college teachers based on the duration of experience.

(Ho7) There will be no significant difference in the mental health of male and female college teachers.

(Ho8) There will be no significant difference in the mental health of rural and urban college teachers.

(Ho9): There will be no significant difference in the mental health of college teachers based on the duration of experience.

(Ho10) There will be no significant difference in the attitude towards the ICT of male and female college teachers.

(Ho11) There will be no significant difference in the attitude towards ICT of rural and urban college teachers.

(Ho12) There will be no significant difference in attitude towards the ICT of college teachers based on the duration of experience.

(Ho13) There will be no significant relationship between teaching effectiveness and the perception of organizational climate of college teachers.

(Ho14) There will be no significant relationship between teaching effectiveness and the mental health of college teachers.

(Ho15) There will be no significant relationship between teaching effectiveness and attitude towards the ICT of college teachers.

(Ho16) There will be no significant relationship between the perception of organizational climate and mental health of college teachers.

(Ho17) There will be no significant relationship between the perception of organizational climate and attitude towards ICT of college teachers.

(Ho18) There will be no significant relationship between mental health and attitude towards ICT of college teachers.

C.5. Significance of the study:

At present in Assam, higher education is expanding and growing rapidly. The number of colleges and enrolment in these colleges is increasing. But due to a lack of quality higher education, Assam is facing challenges (Bora, 2013). Hence, to meet with such challenges of higher education in Assam and implementing the different schemes in college-level effective teachers are must be needed. The study is confined only to the college teachers (Degree College) as the transition from school to college is a significant milestone in the life of students, so the teaching professionals has to face multiple challenges of producing better citizens. For this, the teacher has to keep themselves abreast with knowledge exposure and dynamism. The effectiveness of teachers in a classroom setting is the most crucial factor for affecting the academic progress of the student **(Dutta, et al. 2017)**. So, there exists a considerable need for the teacher to be effective to carry out the desirable changes in learner's behaviour. It is therefore of immense significance to identify and discover some dimensions which have the potential to facilitate or inhibit effective teaching. In this study, the investigator attempts to sort out some of the effectiveness dimensions which may affect teaching performance in either positive aspect or negative aspect. The study is significant as it will facilitate the process of professional development, a better understanding of achieving the effectiveness of teachers which is the most challenging issue for academic, administrative and overall enhancement of the organization. Keeping in view on all these the present study was conducted to study the effectiveness of teaching with special reference of college teachers.

In an organization, the climate is one of the most important factors, as it often acts as a determining aspect of the achievement and failure of the whole organization. While conducting their services, they try to create a balance between the structural, personal, group and cultural systems of the organization. Without teaching, effective learning outcomes and educational goals can never be attained. The organizational environment of an institution is one of the prominent factors that influence the performance level of teachers. There is an intimate relationship between teaching effectiveness and the perception of organizational climate **(Babu & Kumari, 2013)**; so this study will be useful to identify the prevailing climate of the college and its correlation with the effectiveness of teachers. Further, it may also help the college administrators in realizing the importance of effectiveness in the workplace and thereby providing directions for creating a congenial working atmosphere for teachers. Besides, this study also provides a rationale for change and possible directions for achieving the increased effectiveness of teaching. Hence, an actual and systematized study is required in this respect.

Aside from their competency requirements, teachers also have different responsibilities brought by their different roles. Looking into the present scenario of the teacher in a third world country like India, the teacher suffers from many constraints **(Bauer, et al., 2007; Samad, et.al, 2010; Liu & Onwuegbuzie, 2012)**. Most recently, it is seen that college teachers are being occupied in various social and governmental activities like census, election, etc. and miscellaneous other activities. Mental constraints are an acute cause of the mental health problems which emerge due to these various conditions. So, in the present scenario, maintaining the proper mental health of college teachers is the most questionable topic for consistently delivering higher-order performance in the workplace. **Katoch, (2017)** assessed that mental health status affects the teaching performance of the teachers. Supporting this point, an attempt has been made to examine whether there exists any relationship between teaching effectiveness and mental health. So, there is a necessity to focus on the well-being of teacher educators and its possible impact on their teacher effectiveness. The study also endeavours to find out if there exists any difference in mental health consequences based on gender; locality; and duration of the experience. The present study seeks to throw light on the mental health of college teachers. **Panda & Patra (2017)** stated that the level of mental health of teacher can affect his working condition as well as his perception of organizational climate. In general concept, the teacher must have an adequate organizational climate to enjoy mental health. Therefore, being aware of the mental health of teachers in an organization matters very much in the educational system.

Another certain attribute, which affects teacher effectiveness greatly is in developing and maximizing the benefits of ICT in the teaching-learning process. Research by **Sulton (2006)** also shows that ICT enables effective teaching-learning strategies. Especially in colleges, university-level greater intensity of ICT innovations is being implemented to make the effective teaching-learning process. Today new generation's college-going students are living in the digital era as they have so many e-learning platforms in their hands. To satisfy the needs of learners, teachers must require up-to-date knowledge and skills of educational technology. The teachers face a multitudinous number of challenges in their daily classroom teaching to create a new generation. Implementation of ICT can be worthless until teachers develop positive attitudes toward new technologies. Research indicates that the benefit of technology implementation in educational settings mostly relays on teacher's attitudes toward technology use **(Albirini, 2006; Baylor & Ritchie, 2002; Kalogiannakis, 2010)**. There needs to be a balance between using technology and traditional methods of teaching and learning to bring effectiveness in their teaching. On the other hand, it is important to evaluate teachers' attitudes towards ICT and their technical competence as ICTs are being implemented in different government colleges.

The use of ICT affects the performance of students and teachers in the classroom. Hence, as a part of the significance of the study, it must try to throw the light on the aspects of attitude towards the use of information technology and how it is related to teaching. Significantly, the contribution of information technology towards the field of education system helps the teacher to make the teaching-learning process more dynamic and fruitful. The act of teaching along with teachers' favourable mental health, conducive environment, and positive attitude towards ICT and technology competence enforces the teacher to enhance the effectiveness of the teaching and learning process.

The investigator is more convinced that teacher's mental health, organisational climate, and ICT innovation need no longer be neglected in research efforts directed towards a study of exploring the effectiveness of college teachers. The reason is obvious, conceptually they appear to influence the teaching effectiveness but their influence has not yet been empirically studied adequately. This being another reason, the investigator undertakes the present study which attempts to investigate whether the variables organisational climate, mental health and attitude towards information technology correlated with teaching effectiveness of college teachers. Therefore, any research exploring the personal qualities which affect teachers' effectiveness is worthy of pursuit. Thus it is essential to investigate the impact of their attitude and competencies towards ICT in determining the success of the educational system. Studies carried out by former researchers on the various correlated issues of teaching effectiveness, helps the investigator in understanding the gravity of the issue. Likewise, the present investigator selected a few variables related to teaching effectiveness and takes the help of an interlinked model for the empirical verification of the study and it is hoped that this model will add novelty in the study.

The researchers and educationists all over the World, including the Indian researchers, were very much curious about the researches on *Teaching Effectiveness and related Characteristics.* As various studies and research have been conducted internationally and nationally to study teaching effectiveness and related characteristics of the secondary, higher secondary school teachers, only a few studies are also conducted in Assam related to teaching effectiveness and related variables of college teachers.

However, no such attempt is carried out regarding college-level teachers in Guwahati (Kamrup District) in the state of Assam till now. Moreover, studies on mental health, organisational climate, and attitude towards ICT of college teachers and their correlation with each other were almost non-existent.

So, there is a research gap on the multivariate and complex interactions on the issue of teaching effectiveness regarding the concerned variables like mental health, organisational climate, and attitude towards ICT of college teachers. It points to the need for a multivariate study having several independent variables that have great importance in the present time.

Considering all this, the investigator decided to undertake this study. Although there are several antecedent variables of teaching effectiveness, the investigator decided to work on limited and selected variables that have psychological importance. These were: organisational climate, mental health and attitude towards ICT.

C.6. Scope of the study:

- ➤ The teachers working in the provincialized degree colleges comprising only arts and science stream affiliated to Gauhati University were selected for the present study.
- ➤ The study is limited to 548-degree college teachers only due to scarcity of time, money and human resources.
- ➤ The study is confined to only three independent variables gender (male/female), locality (rural/urban) and duration of experience (1-10 years, 10-20 years and above 21 years).

- The study is limited to dependent variables i.e. teaching effectiveness, organizational climate, mental health and attitude towards ICT.
- This study is restricted to only two districts of Assam: Kamrup (Rural) and Kamrup (Metropolitan).

C.7. Proposed model of the study:

Research has indicated that several factors are contributed to predicting teaching effectiveness. But based on the relevance of the study; the investigator has put forwarded a model which signifies three variables as antecedents of teaching effectiveness. These variables are separate but interlinked. These are organizational climate, mental health and attitude towards ICT. But, here it is accepted that there may have some other variables under each of them, yet it may not be feasible to include all of them in a single study. That is why, the investigator decided to scale down the study to the present form, which may represent the relationship of four main variables under study.

To represent teaching effectiveness, the investigator used the teacher effectiveness scale, comprising six different dimensions of teaching effectiveness.

To represent organizational climate, the investigator used a self-devised questionnaire with six subscales i.e. physical environment, library facilities, and reward system, relationship with colleagues, support system and academic climate.

The researcher also applies a self-devised questionnaire of attitude towards information technology for college teachers with a combination of three dimensions i.e. productivity of teaching, usefulness or students' and teachers' interest and acceptance.

Another tool the employee's mental health inventory also used for the given study.

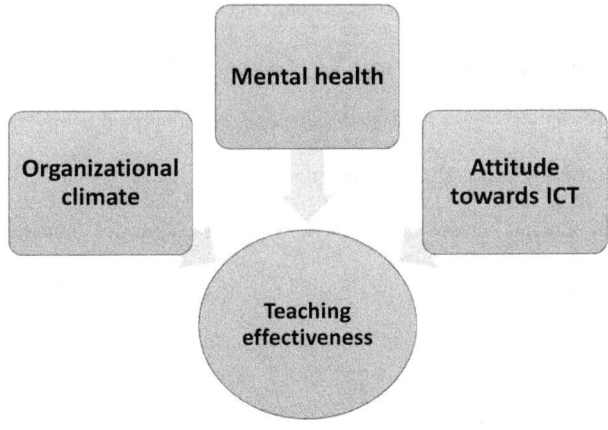

Fig.C.7: Proposed model for teaching effectiveness

The study is designed to assess the validity of this model. Very specifically, the investigator attempted to investigate whether teaching effectiveness is correlated with the other three variables or they tend to separate each other. The investigator also tries to examine and compare each of the variables based on some independent variables among the college teachers working in degree colleges in Kamrup district, Assam.

C.8. Operational definitions of the key concepts:

Teaching Effectiveness: Effective teaching is an evaluation process that involves not only being proficient with teaching practices but also several approaches to facilitate positive changes in the workplace. For this study and in keeping with the correct practice, the terms 'teaching effectiveness' and 'teacher effectiveness' were used synonymously. In the present study, the researcher has used the term teaching effectiveness to mean the effectiveness of teaching delivered by the teacher in the following dimensions such as the ability of the teachers to use knowledge, skill, and behaviours to create an effective learning environment in the classroom, personal and professional qualities, etc. It is defined with the help of a scale, entitled **Teacher Effectiveness Scale (Shallu Puri and S.C. Gakhar).** The scale measures six different dimensions of teaching aspects. These dimensions are mentioned below:

- Academic and professional knowledge
- Preparation and presentation of the lesson plan, classroom management
- Attitude towards students, parents, colleagues, head of the institute
- Use of motivation, reward and punishment and all-round development of students
- Feedback accountability
- Personal qualities

The tool was used to study the teaching effectiveness of college teachers where high scores indicated higher level of effectiveness.

Organizational Climate: In this study, the investigator uses the term "organisational climate" to elaborate on the enduring quality of the internal and external environment of the institution which is experienced by its college teachers. It also refers to the interpersonal relations within the members of the organization and also the collective perceptions, behaviour, attitude of its members that may influence the behaviour of the workers. Regarding the present study, it is defined with the help of a **self-devised questionnaire with six subscales**. The scales are given below:

- Physical environment
- Library facilities
- Reward system
- Relationship with colleagues
- Support system and
- Academic climate

High scores in this Questionnaire individually in the six domains as well as a whole, indicate highly favourable perception of organizational climate, whereas low scores indicate unfavourable organizational climate.

Mental Health: The term mental health is a feature of the general concept of physical, psychological and social health. It refers to a balanced state of mind and possession of a positive attitude. For the present study, mental health is operationally defined as the state of mental pleasure, lacking psycho-physiological complaints, healthy values that determine a person's overall level of personal effectiveness. In the context of the present study, mental health mean scores of teachers working in Degree College will be obtained through **mental health inventory (Jagadish)** which is designed to assess the mental health of personals working in different organisations.

Here too, higher scores indicate satisfactory levels of mental health whereas, low scores indicate moderate mental health status.

Attitude towards Information and Communication Technology: In this study, **Attitude towards ICT** define as a predisposition of a person to respond positively or negatively towards computers and related technologies. It affects everything the person does with the computer and reflects what experience the user has and is hence a determining factor of the user's behaviour towards computers. Attitude towards using new technology for the present study refers to the scores obtained by the self-devised questionnaire of Attitude towards Information Technology for college teachers with a combination of three dimensions. The dimensions are mentioned below-

- The productivity of teaching
- The usefulness of students and

➤ Teacher's interest and acceptance

Here, teachers who secured high scores in the Attitude Scale, were assumed as having highly favourable attitude towards the ICT and vice versa.

College Teachers: The term college teacher used in this study refers to the teachers working in government degree colleges affiliated to Gauhati University. The teaching experience of the college teachers covered in this study is divided into three groups (1-10 years, 10-20 years and above 21 years).

CHAPTER: 2
REVIEW OF RELATED LITERATURE

INTRODUCTION:

According to Best (2008)- A literature review is a systematic study designed to link the past studies carried out by various researchers to the proposed research topic and to solve some problems with the help of most promising methods to bridge the gap between the two. In any scientific psychological research, the significance of the review of related literature or related studies cannot be rebuffed. Research in any field ensures a greater understanding and exploration of the unknown concepts. Familiarity with the related literature develops an insight to enhance and consolidate knowledge of what has already been done in a particular field. Such literature provides an integral part of the entire research process which minimizes the chance of unintentional duplication or repetitions of well-established findings.

Familiarities with forgoing studies serve as a premise for present studies which facilitates a better perspective for further research. Therefore, for having some innovative ideas about current problems the researchers must acquaint with prior information prevailing to one's specific interest. An investigator needs to make an intensive search of all relevant studies from ample sources like relevant research journals, thorough and prudent study of various books, research papers and educational reviews, indexes, encyclopedias, doctoral dissertations, articles, reviews of previous work done on a particular area, abstracts, etc. based on the area of interest under investigations as well as suggestions of supervisor also. Moreover, emerging trends of advanced technology pave a new strength for a researcher to access the online library, e-journal through the internet about the topic under consideration.

Here an attempt has been made to grasp an all-inclusive glimpse of past research that appears to be pertinent with the specific problem of the present topic of investigation. The literature of the last 20 (twenty) years has been reviewed extensively (1999 to 2019). Depending on the nature of the independent and dependent variables of the present research, this chapter gives a review of the studies conducted in India and outside of itbased on the following headings:-

1) Studies related to teaching effectiveness based on gender, locality, and teaching experience.

2) Studies associated with mental health based on gender, locality, and teaching experience.

3) Studies related to the organizational climate based on gender, locality, and teaching experience.

4) Studies related to ICT based on gender, locality, and teaching experience.

5) Studies showing interrelations between teaching effectiveness, mental health, organizational climate, and ICT.

Studies related to teaching effectiveness based on gender, locality, and teaching experience:

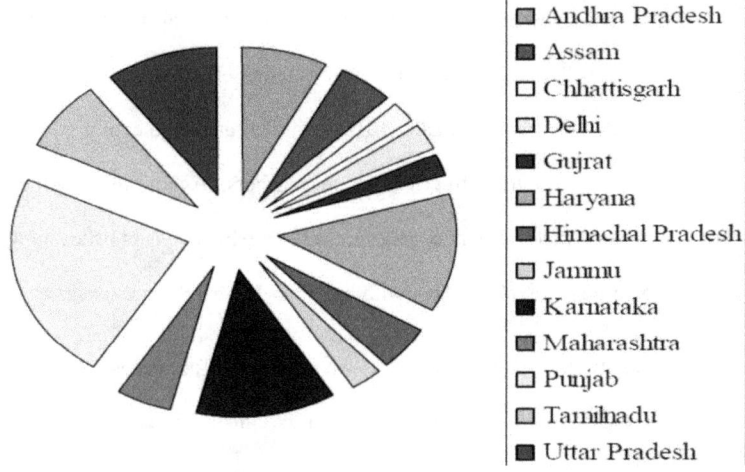

Fig.2 (i): Represents research on teacher effectiveness based on Indian studies

The above figure shows that the Indian states like Punjab, Haryana, and Karnataka the contributions is very remarkable (see Fig.2.1). Still, primarily very few related literature studies were found from the state of Assam on teaching effectiveness with some of the different variables.

➢ **Kumari & Rani (2015)** conducted a study to determine the differentiation in the effectiveness of teachers for gender and type of schools. Findings indicate that although the mean value of female teachers is moderately larger than male teachers; but there exist non-significant variations between them. Similarly, it was observed that Private secondary school teacher's teaching effectiveness is more than government school teachers.

- **Rani and Devi (2015)** tried to determine the outcome of male/female, govt/private school and teaching experience of 150 senior secondary teachers. The teachers were surveyed randomly from the Sonepat district of Haryana. The sample consists of both gender from government and private senior secondary school. The result revealed that teacher effectiveness is no way affected by gender. But a significant difference is found connecting both types of school teachers on the effectiveness of teachers. Again, the findings of the study suggest that teachers are more effective with 10 years of teaching experience as a comparison to teachers with less than 10 years' experience.

- **Kalita (2012)** studied to assess teacher effectiveness with certain personal, professional as well as institutional variables such as qualification, sex, training, teaching experience, age, etc. A few secondary level schools (only fifteen schools) with a sample strength of 50 teachers (thirty-four females and sixteen males) in **Guwahati** of **Kamrup district** has been selected for this purpose. Detailed observations were taken from each teacher in the form of a self-reporting inventory named Teachers effectiveness Questionnaires (TEQ) (consisting of 18 items). Furthermore, teaching effectiveness reveals some unavoidable aspects like the training of teachers which has a visible impact on the teaching-learning process. However, educational qualification and teaching experience are also considered as an important requirement for teaching effectiveness. In the study, female teachers' effectiveness showed high.

- **Pachaiyappan and Raj (2014)** tried to determine the effectiveness of both secondary and higher secondary teachers concerning gender, locality, arts/science, teaching experience as well. The sample consisted of 150 teachers.

Results revealed no dissimilarities among gender in their teaching effectiveness. The researcher also examined that more than 15 years' experienced teachers' effectiveness is high in their teaching in comparison to their counterparts. Similarly, teachers from urban areas hold an upper hand as compared to those of rural areas.

- **Tyagi (2013)** conducted a study to determine the perception of secondary school teachers concerning different dimensions (Knowledge, Organization, Leading, Professionalism, Clarity and Presentation, and Enthusiasm) of teaching effectiveness. The findings highlighted the following things clearly:

    i) It was reported that the effectiveness of urban teacher has a high measure than that of rural teachers.

    ii) The organization dimension has an influential impact on the marital status of secondary school teachers. Unmarried teachers who scored higher cognizance than married teachers.

    iii) Professionalism dimension of teaching effectiveness exerted an impact on the social background and qualification of teachers. In sum, the overall findings depict the picture that teachers are highly motivated by different elements of teaching effectiveness.

- **Kumar (2016)** conducted a study by applying the normative survey method to determine teacher effectiveness among 300 higher secondary teachers. The sample was considered for the investigation only to the higher secondary teachers from different schools in Vellore district, Tamilnadu. An instrument consisting of 60 items namely Teacher Effectiveness Scale by Umme Dixit (1993) which was formulated and approved by the researcher to assess the Teacher Effectiveness.

The conclusions of the analysis indicated no considerable distinction in teaching effectiveness irrespective of both the sexes.

- **Bhat (2017)** studied the effects of the B.Ed. training program in relation to their sexes, type of institute and stream. No significant difference was found in interpersonal relations. It was observed that after the perseverance of B.Ed. training, teaching effectiveness enhanced remarkably. Further, the study depicts the significant consequence of gender on teaching effectiveness due to the impact of the training program. Also, the type of institute and stream is not regulated by the teaching effectiveness with the training of the pupil teachers. The result of the study suggests the productive implementation of teacher education training program in an exceptional way.

- **Malik & Malik (2014)** conducted a study to compare males & females along with rural & urban teachers for teaching effectiveness. The overall sample collected from 600 Participants in Rohtak, India through a random sampling technique. This quantitative study has a survey-type, descriptive design. In terms of the contrast level of teaching effectiveness between genders, the conclusions of the study show that there is a vital association in both genders. Besides that, no gender differences were found in terms of the locality as the community teachers have almost the identical approach regarding teaching effectiveness.

- **Kauts & Chechi (2014)** conducted a study and findings indicated that teaching experience interpreted as a contributing factor towards the performance of teachers. Hence, it elucidated clearly that teachers with more experience expose a higher level of efficacy in teaching. Thus, the results also supported that there is no relationship between school type, emotional intelligence, and teaching experience, on the perception of the efficacy of secondary school teachers.

- **Kumar and Kaur (2017)** found significant differences between gender as well as locality regarding their effectiveness in teaching. The output showed significant assimilation for both genders. Further, it implies that there was no similarity in terms of perception toward the organizational climate for those rural and urban respondents. Besides, this study revealed a positive interest in the perception of organizational climate on teacher effectiveness. Finally, the result highlighted that a conducive institutional climate had a more significant positive effect on a 'high' level of effectiveness.

- **Malik & Sharma (2013)** studied to find out the association between effectiveness and professional commitment among 300 secondary school teachers randomly selected from these 36 schools of Rohtak District of Haryana State, India. The result of the study explores that the sex of teachers does not influence significantly in the case of both teaching effectiveness and professional commitment. But the study suggests male teachers are a little more effective and committed towards the profession. Further, it also depicts that teachers in remote areas feel more professional hindrance as compare to urban areas but their teaching effectiveness identifies as satisfactory. The study also reveals a significant interface between Teaching Effectiveness and Professional commitment of Secondary School Teachers.

- **Dash & Barma (2016)** conducted study only 100 secondary school teachers from West Bengal, India were taken for the research purpose through the descriptive survey method. The out-turn highlights that although there is no prominent dissimilarity based on gender, stream, training status, teaching experience, and qualification. However, from the study, it is evident that the mean score affects some areas of study like sex and teaching experience. The higher mean score indicates that female teachers are comparatively better in comparison to male teachers. Likewise, highly qualified teachers above 5-10 years show a higher level of effectiveness than that of another group of teachers. It is also interesting evident from the means that untrained teachers and rural school teacher's effectiveness is higher regarding trained and urban school teachers which are not generally expected in any educational endeavor.

- **Onyekuru & Ibegbunam (2013)** found that the majority of teacher experience a mediocre level of teaching effectiveness. Hence, result signifies that gender does not influence the potency of teachers. The present finding explains the fact that more experience teacher contributes extraneous aptitude skill towards the journey of effectiveness. Finally, present study concludes that teaching experience and qualification have a greater influence on effectiveness of secondary school teachers.

- **Thirumavalavan & Balakrishnan (2013)** conducted a study to find out how gender and locality is associated with the effectiveness of 300 teacher educators, working in B.Ed. colleges affiliated to Tamilnadu Teachers Education University, Chennai, located in Namakkal District of Tamilnadu. The outcomes showed majority respondents were able to draw a priority line regarding their efficiency in teaching (preeminent level of performance in terms of all the dimensions in teacher effectiveness among teacher educators). Besides that male and female had no remarkable consequence for teacher efficiency. Further it was inferred that urban teacher education colleges implied greater level of effectiveness in comparison to rural areas.

- **Arya & Singh (2016)** found that gender does insignificant effect on effectiveness of teachers. The crucial findings of the present study also signify that no distinction exists in teacher effectiveness for stream, senior secondary and secondary level and length of experience in teaching.

- **Kumari & Padhi (2014)** conducted a study among 200 samples from rural and urban schools of Bilaspur district, Chattisgarh, India through stratified random sampling method. The data were statistically analysed by applying frequency percentage, mean, SD, t-test and ANOVA. Result revealed that teacher's effectiveness did not get affected by the gender but types of inhibition played important role towards the gateway of effectiveness among teachers. It was established that female of urban and rural areas did not put significant effect on effectiveness. The study also observed that gender as well as types of habitation has significant interaction effect on teacher effectiveness.

- **Kaur & Sharma (2015)** studied to assess the various interactions of occupational stress, teaching experience, gender on teaching effectiveness. The result revealed that both male and female teachers with different teaching experience had almost same level of competency. Finding concluded that teacher effectiveness did not get affected by occupational stress.

- **Buela & Joseph (2015)** has chosen total number of 58 high school teachers whose chronological age ranges from 31 -60 years from Government Schools in Gulbarga was selected through purposive sampling method. The result exhibited that there is no statistically significant difference regarding age, sexes and qualification of the respondents. On the other hand experienced teachers performed effectively in teaching profession than that of others (F=3.66; p<0.05).

Studies related to mental health based on gender, locality, stream and teaching experience:

➢ **Rani & Singh (2012)** carried out 100 primary school teachers by using Probability sampling method. The result of the study found average level of mental health among school teachers. Besides, it was analysed no significant impact of gender with regards to mental health among teachers. Also, no significant difference was found regarding mental health amidst the genders regarding types of schools.

➢ **Baro & Panda (2014)** found no significant distinction among genders about both mental health and job satisfaction. But, the obtained analysis found that mean value of female teachers is higher than male on mental health and job satisfaction. Conclusively, it has observed that the mental healths of the teachers are correlated positively with job satisfaction in different conditions.

➢ **Mankani & Yenagi (2012)** conducted a study comprised of total 180 working and non-working women to assess the mental health status of both the categories. The results revealed that the working women are significantly differing with non-working women regarding mental health dimensions. While, the mental health of working women in urban areas found to be better mental health conditions. Besides that, negative but significant correlation was found in term of family size among the working women about mental health status.

➢ **Kumar, Kumar & Kumari (2013)** conducted a study to compare the mental health of 160 teachers based on male/female and rural/urban. The finding of the study revealed that male/female, rural/urban teachers did not point out any distinction concerning their mental health status.

- **Dagar & Mathur (2016)** carried out to explore the mental health of 600 government and non-government school teachers. The study was collected from 600 teachers i.e. (300 government, 300 non-government school teachers) teaching in different schools of District (Hisar, Kurukshetra, Rohtak and Faridabad) of Haryana. Result indicated that male teachers mental health was significantly differ from female teachers of Haryana. It also found that male teachers occupied better physiological health than the female teachers. On the other hand, Type of school has no impact on the teachers' health condition.

- **Pathak (2015)** conducted a study to identify the comparison between occupational stress and mental health comprising 100 (50male &50female) primary school teachers in Rajkot city (Gujarat). Result revealed that occupational stress and mental health differ for both genders. While positive interrelations were there between occupational stress and mental health.

- **Panda & Patra (2017)** conducted a research by using random sampling in selecting twenty school teachers from Krishnanagar-II, block of Nadia district of West Bengal as a sample for study. Researchers had adopted R.C.E. Mental Health Scale, consisted with 60 items (5 point Likart Type) for collecting of data. Study revealed that, location, gender and stream of teaching do not influence the health of Bengali medium school teachers in Nadia district of West Bengal. Difference was there among demographic variables (i.e. locale, gender & stream of teaching), still the teachers had good psychological health status. The present research also recommended doing more research to identify the specific factors by which, mental health of school teachers will implant productively.

- **Galgotra (2013)** studied to find out the mental health of 250 teachers from Jammu and Kashmir with regards to the triple effect of type of teacher, gender, and job satisfaction. Results of the study indicate that both types of teacher and satisfaction towards work both have interaction effect on the mental health. Likewise, the analysis signifies that government teacher's mental health status are better .Further, it also clears that teachers with higher level of satisfaction towards job are more stable related to their mental health.

- **Mohana (2013)** conducted a study by applying normative survey method among 640 teachers to measure the influence of independent variables such as teaching level and teaching experience on the mental health. The psychological tool namely, mental health inventory has been administered to a stratified random sample selected teachers working at different levels in various educational institutions in Cuddalore district, Tamil Nadu, India. Result implies no significant difference in terms of both the teaching level and experience on the mental-physical health of school teachers.

- **Manikandan (2012)** conducted a study to identify the effect of gender and organization on occupational health of 805 teachers whose chronological age ranges from 23-55 years. The study belonging to higher secondary school/college, Kerala. Finally, the results revealed that gender and institution both had remarkable effects on the components of occupational health. It is observed that in college sector the mental health percentage of female teachers has scored more in comparison to male. But, comparatively in school setting male teachers possessed optimum level of mental health condition (60.11, n=116) than females (60.11, n=116).

- **Aliakbari (2015)** conducted a descriptive-explanatory study aimed to examine the influence that work satisfaction had on the mental health of teachers. The research sample was determined 332 (140 women and 192 men) teachers by using Krejcie and Morgan method in the province of Mazandaran, Iran. The data was collected using questionnaires with open and close questions. The results from the obtained coefficients showed a meaningful positive interrelation between work satisfaction and mental health of the studied teachers. Further, the findings concluded that among those two variables women possessed stronger interaction than men counterparts.

- **Mishra (2018)** carried out to identify the mental health of 200 secondary school teachers in connection with gender, management and educational qualification of Murshidabad district, West Bengal. The result revealed prominent distinction in mental health regarding gender and management alteration. Hence, educational qualification did not play any action in framing the mental health of teachers. The paper strictly recommended enhancing the health condition of teachers to avoid academic distractions.

- **Gorsy, Panwar & Kumar (2015)** studied the differential influence of gender and locality on personal psychical health of 100 teachers, Haryana. The study showed significant gender differences on the psychical health of government school teachers ($t = 2.39$; $p \leq .02$). Additionally, important distinction existed between localities regarding health conditions ($t = -6.46$; $p \leq .001$). Descriptive data analysis revealed that male teachers tend to perform better than their female analogue. Finally, the study reported that teachers concerning urban area displayed good quality of mental health in comparison to rural area.

- **Maheswara (2017)** carried out a study to investigate the issue of health status considering gender, locality, language and non-language teaching of high school teacher. Data were collected randomly from 130 teachers of both genders and habitant from Kurnool district, Andhra Pradesh. The mental health survey data were gathered by mental health inventory. The study implied non-significant distinction in mental health in regards to habitant as well as language and non-language teaching. However, from the study it was evident that mental health got affected by gender and type of school. The higher mean score showed that teachers comprising remote areas possessed adequate mental health in contrast to urban areas. Additionally, Non- language teaching teachers mean scores consumed in higher position as compare to language teaching teachers. Study also highlighted that female teachers contributed favorable health condition to transform better life. Moreover, majority of government high school teachers' were able to tie a line of priorities towards sound mental health.

- **Pachaiyappan & Raj (2014)** found gender distinction in terms of mental health. It means mental health of female teachers' specified better in contrast to male teachers. Moreover, teachers of higher secondary school showed considerable mental health than the secondary school teachers. There exists non-significant gender differences were found concerning the location and stream of teaching. Based on the type of management, mental health of teachers differ significantly i.e. Government school teachers (m=191.63) felt maximal mental health.

- **Marta et al. (2015)** studied the stressful working condition and mental health consequences of 37 selected schoolteachers. Results indicated that majority respondents were able to tie an edge of priorities in frustrating working situations in respect to sufficient salary. It was observed that teachers with stressful working conditions showed adverse influence on the health status of teachers. Teachers reported to enhance good interpersonal relationship, cohesion towards working conditions for ultimate promotion of healthy well-being in the workplace. Additionally, suggestions were made to implement the policies and measures to enhance the recognition of teaching professions which devoted both in mental health and professional performance.

- **Prathima & Kulsum (2013)** found that teachers with higher extent of social intelligence had acquired superior mental health condition. The results indicated significant gender difference based on mental health of secondary school teachers.
- **Bappan (2018)** conducted a study of 100 government and private college teachers out of which 50 are from government and 50 from private aided colleges from Kalaburgi district of North Karnataka state. Result showed that both government and private aided college teachers greatly influenced in mental health of college faculties. This result indicated form the study that government college teachers possessed higher quantity of mental-physical health in contrast to private aided college teachers. According to the mean score, it was identified that teachers belonging to science stream displayed sound mental health than that of Arts and Commerce faculties. Hence, it also clearly accepted that there was significant impact of educational stream such as Arts, Commerce and Science on mental health among teachers of Government private aided colleges.
- **Rahaman (2017)** studied the mental health consequences of 100 teachers' from private B.Ed training institute within the district of Murshidabad, India. The aim investigated the mental health condition relating to gender and locality. The

researchers were found no significant gender as well as locality distinction in respect to mental health consequences.

- **Pandhi and Rajendra (2010)** found that organizational climate and mental and physiological health of teachers were correlated to demographical variables. It also found that health condition of teachers was significantly differing concerning both rural and urban high schools. The findings concluded that organizational climate was not influence on the health status of teachers.

- **Basu (2009)** found male teachers mental health significantly better as compared to their female colleagues. It also concluded that, female teachers are faced with the multiple burdens of double responsibilities –family and work, leading to greater stress and hence poorer mental health.

- **Rathee (2017)** conducted a study to examine the difference between 90 regular and contractual teachers regarding mental health. For data collection, the investigator used the 'Employee's Mental Health Inventory' developed by Jagdish (2001). Data analyses were done by applying Mean, SD and t-test. Results revealed that gender had significant difference regarding mental health. Further findings show that Age and teaching experience also has an impact on the health of the teachers.

- **Khatun (2013)** studied to find out teachers burnout regarding some personal variables sex, age group, experience, and subject taught, training variation, and management variation. The study revealed significant difference in gender, age group, experience, subject and variation of training but there is no significant difference found in management variation of teacher burnout at secondary level.

- **Dewan, et al. (2009)** found low score in mental health of female, in comparison to male counterparts. Females are worked more in maintaining households, raising family, caring out economically productive activities in marketing and so they work more hours than do their husbands.

> **Gangwar, et al. (2004)** studied on mental health status and adjustment of public school teacher and govt. school teacher. They found no significant gender difference in respect of their mental health.

> **Pradhan (2016)** conducted a study to investigate the mental health condition of secondary teachers of Sikkim. Study found, significant gender dissimilarity concerning mental health. Similarly educational qualifications and management variation of the schools were. But teachers' mental health condition was not influenced by their teaching experience.

> **Yin-Ling (2006)** conducted a study and found that most of the female teachers were in a dilemma of how to perform and synchronize the social and family responsibilities well, which has been a heavy trouble on their mental and physical health.

Studies related to the organizational climate based on gender, locality, stream and teaching experience:

> **Tiwri (2014)** carried out a study to analyse the organisational climate amongdifferent groups of teaching staff in Higher Education Institutions. The present study also tried to find if there exist any variations of the perception of organizational climate in different groups of teachers. The result indicated that among 22 items of organisational climate almost 13 items reflected fairy good level in higher education institutions. Further, based on the average mean score and percentage score, it has been found among the various categories as 4.07 (76.75%) for group a (University Professors & College Principals),3.92 (73%)

for group B (University and College Associate Professors), and 3.85 (71.25%) for group C (University and College Assistant Professors) reciprocally. The average mean score and percentage of the overall organisational climate has been computed at 3.95 (73.75%). The result of the study concluded that the organisational climate of the higher education institutions is in a satisfactory level of perception (fairly good) and the variation among the different groups of teachers does not exist which are verified with the hypothesis.

- **Kumar & Kaur (2017)** studied to find out the relationship between teacher effectiveness and organizational climate based on male-female and rural-urban Engineering college teachers. The results revealed that there exists significant relationship between teacher effectiveness and organizational climate of engineering college teachers. Urban area teachers have better perception of organizational climate than rural area teachers.

- **Kumar & Singh (2015)** conducted a study to hypothesize the relationship would be mediated by adjustment pattern and organizational climate regarding gender and areas. The samples were chosen randomly through probability method of sampling. The analysis of the study remarked negative and insignificant relationship between adjustment and the perception of organizational climate of secondary school teachers. Majority of the subjects also stated that although female teachers scored little high on the perception of organizational climate than the male teachers, still the gender and areas of school did not affect much on organisational climate setting of schools.

- **Manikandan (2014)** carried out a study to examine the impact of organizational climate, length of teaching (2 to 27 years) and sex on work engagement among

101 teachers pertains to Aided, Government school. Results found that work engagement of school teachers is self-contained regarding sex and organizational climate. Moreover, length of teaching and gender of the participants is also found to be significantly correlated with each other on work engagement. It can be realised that male teachers comprising 11 years of teaching experience have an escalation in their engagement of work in comparison to female teachers.

- **Rani & Rani (2014)** conducted a descriptive survey to discover the correlation as well as comparison between job satisfaction and the organisational climate of elementary school teachers. The results identified that job satisfaction and organizational climate both are imperceptibly correlated. It was also found that concerning climate setting and job satisfaction both the genders (male/female) are not significantly coordinated.

- **Mahmudiha (2016)** conducted a survey to pertain the correlation between organizational climate and job performance concerning the variables such as age/ years of service /education level, and gender among 160 randomly selected teachers. According to the result of this research, Spearman correlation coefficient showed favorable significant correlation between organizational climate and the employees performance ($r = 0.365$, $P < 0.001$). Besides, it was perceived as weak and insignificant relationship between ages /years of service and education level with work performance. But, in case of salary and benefits the perceived job performance was confirmed high as the performance of teachers got affected by the increased rate of salary.

- **Maheshbabu, Chengti & Walhinde (2014)** carried out a research to identify the correlation between organisational climate and job anxiety of 100 randomly selected sample from Yadagiri city, North Karnataka, India. The researcher found no gender impact on organisational climate. On the other hand, there was significant influence of gender on job anxiety. The result indicated that female teachers facing higher scored better anxiety than the male teachers (t=15.38, p<0.05). Further, organisational climate and job anxiety was found significantly correlated to each other.
- **Shukla & Mishra (2007)** studied to interpret the perception of organizational climate of both professional and non-professional college's staff members of Madhya Pradesh, India. Findings inculcated that perceptivity of organizational climate among employees of professional and non-professional colleges did not contradict notably to each other. It was noticeable that teaching employee's perception towards organizational climate indicated more desirable comparing with non-teaching employees. Female employees had more positive perception towards organizational settings than male. Study also reported that postgraduate employees comprehended better organisational climate than that of their undergraduate colleagues.
- **Kumar (2015)** studied to evaluate the correlation between job satisfaction and organizational climate variables among teaching /non-teaching staff of various universities. For this study the investigator implied 389 copies of questionnaire to selected universities but finally only 293 questionnaires are filled by the staff members. Positive but significant correlation found between all respondents comprising organizational climate and job satisfaction. Significant differences

also found among teaching /non-teaching staff based on teaching experience on climate setting at F= 430.768.

➢ **Chaithra & Hiremath (2018)** conducted a study in Dharwad and Kalaghatagi taluks of Dharwad district of Karnataka among 150 primary and secondary rural school teachers. Results found that majority (76.67 %) of the respondents perceived as favourable followed by more favourable (22.67 %) and less favourable (0.66 %). The major problems faced by rural school teachers are drinking water, lack of teaching aids, no sufficient building for school, family responsibilities, no playground, less guidance, no toilet rooms, lack of coordination, health problems, unnecessary record enquiry, lack of adjustment difficult to take care of children and lack of freedom for free discussion.

Studies related to attitude towards ICT based on gender, locality, stream and teaching experience:

➢ **Mahajan (2016)** conducted a study to find out the attitude towards the application of ICT in teaching of secondary school teachers. The result showed that only a few teachers had favorable attitude in the direction of technology adaptation in teaching. No significant difference was found between male and female and duration of experience in regards to the attitudes of technology usability in educational purposes.

➢ **Olafare, Festus Oladimeji, Lawrence Olugbade Adeyanju, Fakorede (2017)** conducted a study to investigate 1107 (602 males and 505 females) lecturers attitude toward towards the use of ICT from 10 selected colleges. Lecturers signified favorable attitude in the direction of ICT application. The study showed non-significant gender influence in teacher's attitude. But, significant difference was established amidst first degree holders and higher degree holders in their attitudes. Findings also revealed significant attitude variation among experienced and less-experienced lectures, as experienced lecturers hold up prominent attitude towards ICT in contrast to less-experienced fellow.

➢ **Langroudi (2015)** studied the factors which influenced the Information and Communication Technology (ICT) usage and implemented awareness in the direction of teachers' points of views among 97 randomly selected samples in Kharazmi University, Iran. The study found no significant difference among the teacher's points of views on their efforts to utilize ICT professionally in teaching-learning process. Significant correlation was also examined among the attitude on use of ICT and age. The teachers from different age ranges focused their efforts to integrate technology pedagogically during the teaching and learning process.

➢ **Samuel (2013)** carried out a study to investigate whether the gender affected the availability, accessibility and the use of ICT among academic institutions. The analysis of data interpreted that gender had insignificant impact on accessibility and usability of ICT facilities. Again, the findings revealed that gender had great impact on the areas of ICT facilities such as, participation with other tertiary faculty members, executing data management services, and performing task more rapidly as well.

➢ **Kandasamy & Shah (2013)** found that most of the people faced moderate level on ICT implication. Likewise, the bulk of the respondents revealed that they used ICT for the purpose like keeping track of student's performance, accessing information and educational materials, preparing lesson plan, doing presentation relevant to topics. It illustrated that most of the teachers had favourable attitude of ICT implementation for educational purposes.

- **Onasanya, Shehu, Oduwaiye & Shehu (2010)** studied the attitude of higher institution lecturers towards inclusion of ICT and also tried to survey the impact on age, area of discipline, gender, or educational experience on application of ICT. The findings showed that gender and academic qualifications of both had not put any incentives on ICT implication in educational settings. Similarly, amazed result found that the less experienced faculties were more agreeable to new confrontation of using ICT facilities than the senior ones. Again, University lecturers possessed more competences and ICT acquisition skills than Polytechnics and colleges of education, respectively.

- **Ganesan & Krishnakumar (2016)** conducted a study to find out the difference between teacher educators' attitude towards ICT and their attitude level regarding gender and locality. Result indicated that preponderance of teacher educators produced propitious attitudes concerning ICT implementation. Findings observed that locality established significant effect on educator's attitude. But it was not conclusively proved that gender had a specific impact on teacher's attitude.

- **Angadi (2014)** studied the difference of influence of gender (male/ female), type of experience (above 10 years/below 10 years) and stream (arts/science) of teacher educators on the attitude towards ICT. Results found the significant role of both gender and stream on the attitude of teachers as the male teacher's attitude level towards ICT showed comparatively higher than female. Additionally, the type of experience did not influence on teacher's attitude in the direction of ICT implementation.

- **Konca, Ozel & Zelyurt (2016)** tried to describe preschool teacher's attitude towards ICT and also analysed the attitude comparing with certain demographic characteristics. Descriptive study was adopted for the study comprising 103 teachers working at kindergartens in city centre of Kırsehir and Malatya. The result showed optimistic attitude regarding teacher's application of technological tool.

- **Nagamani & Muthuswamy (2013)** conducted a study of secondary school teachers capabilities to apply ICT in schools dealing with the factors i.e. male/female, location (rural/semi urban and urban area) and age. Data reported that the utilization of ICT was not affected by the gender. Further, location of school and age group were found statistically significant in the use of ICT. Teachers belonging to urban areas reported that they had more opportunities to access and avail internet services when compared with rural and semi urban schools. Again, younger teachers were technically more advanced than rest of the age Groups. Although, the senior teachers were well acquainted with academic productivity; they confronted lack of training facilities to assimilate computer technology.

- **Onwuagboke & Singh (2014)** studied to find out how faculty members apply internet in the instructional delivery process. The investigator randomly selected 350 lecturers. The result showed significant difference between both the genders of faculty members in respect of internet use. In the same vein, teaching experience had great impact on the frequency of internet use as, less experienced faculty members are more persistent on the internet in contrast to more experienced colleagues.

- **Kumar and Madhumalathi (2016)** studied the Awareness in ICT among 60 B.Ed. teacher training institutions with effective implementation of Education. This study found significant gender difference regarding ICT implication (t=3.14, p<0.05).Male teachers showed optimal awareness for technology adaptation than their female counterparts. Significant difference also established concerning Government/ Aided and Unaided management institution (f=12.36, p, 0.05).

- **Akturk, Izci, Caliskan& Sahin(2015)** conducted a study to figure out the pre-service teachers attitude technology with some predictive variables such as male/female, length of internet use, total number of technical devices possessed among 329 pre-service teachers. Result exhibited that both the genders influences are prominent on pre-service teachers' attitudes in respect to technology. When compared male with female teachers it was established that male teachers had more efficacious attitude towards ICT than that of female pre-service teachers (t=3.678; $p<0.001$). Likewise, study emancipated the positive relationship between the quantity of possessed technological devices and positive attitudes for technology (β=.169), as the greater amount of technology utilization devices increased positive direction towards technology integration.

- **Chandini (2016)** found remarkable distinction regarding the age of teachers **towards** the use of computers. Major outcomes of the study revealed that Teachers below 40 years showed more explicit attitude to use computer effectively in education when compared with teachers of above 40 years. The findings had indications for the teachers to furnish themselves through computer related trainings, assign infrastructural facilities through which they can uplift their potential for better enhancement of educational process.

- **Erdogan** (2010) carried out a study to determine the influence of male/female, length of experience, the duration of manipulation of computer among 1540 teachers. It was found that attitudes differ according to the length of experience and appropriate knowledge of teachers. Significant gender difference also examined regarding total frequency of technology use. Positive and significant correlation also there within experience of teachers and ICT knowledge and also attitude towards internet and computer.

- **Ashok & Prabakaran (2016)** studied to evaluate the manifestation of ICT application and to figure out the knowledge of e-resources among the college members of three autonomous Arts/Science Colleges of Madras. The study also investigated the acceptance of ICT maintenance and also the basic problems of using ICT faced by the faculty members in colleges. Data analysis exhibited majority of faculty members showed positive attitude towards integration of ICT. It was appeared in the result that less quantity of samples impotent with the enhancement of competency and skill relating to ICT.

- **Sridharan & Krishnakumar (2015)** conducted a study to find out the aptitude of teacher educators towards ICT of 300 teacher educators. The results showed significant gender difference in their attitude towards technology, and also for their subject taught. The results also showed non-significant difference in respect to their locality towards ICT application.

Studies showing interrelations between teachings effectiveness, mental health, organizational climate and attitude towards ICT:

- **Singh & Singh (2015)** studied how teaching competence/attitude towards ICT/ teacher effectiveness were related to each other among 100 school teachers. The findings indicated no any direct relationship concerning teaching competence/teacher effectiveness/ attitude towards ICT and among school teaches. It can be concluded that all the three components are not influenced by each other.

- **Sodhi (2012)** found that the secondary school teachers recognising open organizational climate have revealed significantly satisfactory level of teacher effectiveness in comparison to closed type of climate. There is no certain significant difference in effectiveness of teachers regarding male/female, rural/urban, teaching experience groups and streams (science/social science/language).

- **Manikandan (2012)** conducted a research to identify the influence of educational climate and academic qualification on occupational mental health of college teachers in Kerala. The study revealed that organizational climate and academic qualification notably collaborated on occupational mental health and its related components.

- **Ravi (2016)** found no significant difference between the attitudes towards using new technology and teaching effectiveness based on both male/female and teacher's affiliation board. Although the difference was not substantial, it also distinctly indicated from the study that male mean scores show high and they are cautious towards new technology. The study was also highlighted a significant positive association between usage of new technology and teaching effectiveness among male teachers and teacher's affiliation boards.

- **Sethi (2015)** carried out to study the distinction between mental-physical health and teaching effectiveness regarding gender and type of school. Results highlighted that no significant gender and type of school (govt and private school) impact were perceived based on their mental health and teacher effectiveness.

- **Borkar (2013)** conducted a study to find out the interrelation between the effectiveness and stress level among teachers by hypothesizing that there would be no relationship between the two. 1000 teachers from Secondary schools located in different regions of Mumbai, Thane and Raigad areas of Maharashtra were recruited through multistage sampling technique. Findings of the result indicated that less effective teachers puts high effect on stress level in comparison to highly effective group of teachers. The findings further clarified that the female teachers facing significantly higher Stress condition compared to their male counterparts, although the salary and workload were equally implemented among both the categories.

- **Pan & Wu (2015)** found that organizational climate has an impact on the teachers' mental health. Therefore, the study recommended that educational practitioners and administrators should strengthen the whole infrastructure style in universities by stimulating positive and good interpersonal climate, which certainly enhances the efficiency and development of mental health in university faculties.

- **Bala & Bashir (2016)** conducted a study to assess whether the effectiveness of teaching related with work motivation of 200 secondary school teachers (100 male and 100 female) from Kashmir, India. The result showed that effectiveness of teaching and work motivation were not related significantly one another.

- **Kaur (2018)** found that there was no dissimilarity in terms of perception toward teaching effectiveness for those male and female as well as Government and private senior secondary schools respondents. Further no significant distinction in organizational climate settings were worked out in terms of both gender and type of the schools. Besides that effectiveness of teacher and organizational climate are not significantly correlated to one another (t=0.101, P is less than 0.05).

- **Kumar (2010)** conducted a study to determine the competence of teaching among 242 primary school teachers. The results of the study indicated that Organizational climate perception bring significant and positive influence on competence of teaching. The study showed significant correlation between 'Organizational Climate Perception' and 'Teaching Competence' among teachers based on male/female; locality/type of institution/teaching experience, but no interrelation was found between perception of organizational climate and competency of teaching concerning educational qualification.

- **Saun, Gangwani, & Jain (2016)** studied to examine the existing organisational climate of business school and concurrently investigated the overall influence of both the variables. The study showed moderate degree of overall organisational climate among schools, as majority of respondents were able to tie middle line of priorities. Findings also reported strong repercussion of institutional climate on teacher's motivation level. This means that favourable working organizational setting according to the requirements highly motivated the teachers to do their work with full potential and effectively.

- **Kaur (2013)** conducted a study to find out the perception of organizational climate, mental health and occupational stress. The study also tried to examine the relationship between the perception of organizational climate and mental health of teachers working in college of education. Results found significant difference of gender among the teachers based on perception of organizational climate. Correlation was there between the perception of organizational climate and mental health of teachers.

- **Raza (2010)** conducted a study to find out significant relationship between the teaching performance and organizational climate of Degree College teachers. Result identified that most of the teachers showed much better performance rated to open climate than that of paternal or closed climate. Similarly, college teachers opined that behaviours and reaction of staff members related to closed climate was very unsatisfactory which promoted negative effect on their teaching performance. Also, to avoid the destructions of teacher's performance suggestions were formed to promote favourable climate so that the teachers would discuss different academic problems openly without hesitation.

- **Babu & Kumari (2013)** found out that majority respondents belonging to government schools where open climate exist indicates high performance in their effectiveness. It was also highlighted that effectiveness of teachers are significantly differ with organizational climate that means dimension of organizational climate such as open as well as closed climate have a remarkable influence on Teacher Effectiveness.

- **Selamat, Samsu &Kamalu (2013)** conducted a study to evaluate the impact of organisational climate on teaching performance of 37 teachers. The study revealed organisational climate as predominant factor which had great impact on teachers' job performance.

- **Ghosh & Guha (2016)** studied 221 teacher educators in West Bengal to evaluate the perceived organizational climate and status of motivation to work. It was found that perceived organizational climate and level of motivation to work of teacher educators both were not symmetrically assigned in teacher education institutions. Besides, the organizational climate as perceived by teacher educators was not affected on their motivation to work.

- **Riti (2010)** conducted a study to examine the teacher effectiveness of secondary schools regarding gender/locality and also investigated the relationship between teacher effectiveness and school organizational climate of secondary school teachers. The result indicated no significant gender difference in the teacher effectiveness. Location of schools has significant impact on the effectiveness of teachers. Significant relationship was found between teacher effectiveness and organizational climate of secondary school teachers.

- **Goel (2011)** conducted a study to find out the relationship between teacher effectiveness, job satisfaction, personality and mental health of school teachers regarding gender and locality. Result indicated positive and significant correlation between teaching effectiveness and mental health of the school teachers.

- **Bronkhorst, Tummers, Steijn & Vijverberg (2014)** carried out systematic study to assess the correlation between mental health and organizational climate among the working professionals. The study also examined which dimensions of organizational climate were greatly correlated to the mental health of the workers. Findings indicated that organizational climate dimensions such as leadership and supervision established enormous influence on mental health, but participation/communication, placed no or very little effect on mental health issues.

- **Alikhani & Lebadi (2014)** conducted a study to assess the relationship between climate of the organization, organizational justice and health status among the workers of Shahid Beheshti Medical University comprising 190 employees which were selected randomly. Result revealed organizational justice was significantly associated with organizational climate, but no significant attachment was found between organizational climate and organizational justice with mental health condition. Findings also indicated another point that gender played crucial role in organisational justice; however, no significant influence was identified by gender in between mental health and organisational climate setting.

- **Rathee (2016)** carried out a study to differentiate the mental-physiological health and commitment towards organization of school teachers based on gender (female and male) and interaction impact of both the variables. Findings revealed significant association between primary and secondary school teachers regarding mental health but type of school was not influence the organizational commitment of teachers. Result also indicated significant correlation between commitment of organization and mental health status of school teachers.

- **Islahi (2010)** studied the relationship between teaching effectiveness of secondary school teachers with their work motivation and attitude towards information technology. Result revealed that location/ gender/ medium of instruction had no significant influence on teaching effectiveness of secondary school teachers. Positive and substantially significant relationship was found between teaching effectiveness and attitude towards ICT of secondary school teachers.

- **Ruth Oluwatosin Adeyemo, Emmanuel Olusola Adu and Olusesan Adeyemi Adelabu (2015)** conducted a study to examine the position of ICT by inspecting the educators' literacy level of ICT, availability of ICT infrastructures in the field of Technical Colleges. Findings showed that more than 68% of educators were well acquainted with training of technology application and majority of teachers consumed adequate knowledge of new technologies. Again, result explored that 76% of college educators operated ICT assets efficaciously in the province of teaching processes. Further, it was revealed that technical colleges are faced with some difficulties of availability of ICT resources.

- **Adeshina, Tunde Joel, Udoh, Abasido, Ndomi, Benjamin & Aliyu, Muhibeedeen (2013)** found out the interrelationship between the Information Technology skills obtained by Secretarial Teachers and implementation of Internet for improvement of teaching among 250 samples from 58 Accredited in Nigerian Colleges of Education. Result found that there was moderate favourable interrelation between the technology skills and the potential use of internet to retrieve knowledge for efficient teaching. The findings reported the deficiencies of ICT skills of secretarial teachers, which made difficult for them to enable quality and effective classroom delivery technique.

- **Rajeswari & Sree (2017)** studied the influence of gender and the way of handling classes on teaching competence and attitude towards ICT of 500 teacher educators within Chidambaram town in Cuddalore district, Tamilnadu. Results revealed that teacher educators delivered immense extent of competence in teaching. Likewise, favourable attitude showed towards ICT implementation among teacher educators. Data analysis examined significant difference in both teaching competence and attitude towards ICT concerning the way of handling classes. Consequently, gender had specific impact on attitude towards ICT, But not in teaching competence among teacher educators. Results also indicated significant correlation between competency of teaching and attitude towards ICT of teacher educators.

Table 2.1: **Systematic review of literature related to Assam regarding all variables**

Author	Journal/Dissertation/Thesis	Location	Objectives	Findings
Chowdhury (2014)	The Clarion	Assam, India	To study the teacher effectiveness of 250 (male=140, female=110) secondary school teachers with their gender, age, experience & qualification	No significant difference in terms of gender, age, experience & qualification among the secondary school teachers effectiveness.

Kalita & Saha (2013)	PARIPEX- Indian Journal Research	Assam, India	To study the effectiveness of teachers teaching English in the Secondary school regarding gender.	Insignificant gender difference in the effectiveness of teaching; but mean score of male teachers was found to be higher than the female teachers.
Baro (2014)	The Int. Journal of Humanities & Social Studies	Bongaigaon district, Assam	An investigation on mental health especially female teachers regarding rural/urban and management facilities	The study exhibited certain dissimilarity concerning locality. Study also inculcated that urban teachers' health condition was better than the rural areas.
Goswami & Choudhury (2017)	Int. Journal of Applied Research	Kamrup District of Assam	Examined the climate level of different non-govt. teachers' training colleges (B. Ed) with their locality.	Results show that the climate level of these teachers' training institutes is significant and different. The investigators also find that the institutional climate of rural and urban B.Ed. colleges is same.
Baro & Panda (2014)	Abhinav National Monthly Refereed Journal of Research in Commerce &	Bangaigaon, Assam, India	To study the mental health and job satisfaction of male & female primary school teachers and also to investigate the relationship of mental and job	No significant difference was found between male and female primary school teachers regarding mental health and job satisfaction. The result also revealed no significant relationship

	Management,		satisfaction of the teachers.	between mental health and job satisfaction of primary school teachers.
Devi & Talukdar (2018)	International Journal of Research in Social Sciences & Humanities	Kamrup District of Assam	To explore the effectiveness of college teachers about their mental health regarding their gender (male and female) and locality (rural and urban).	Result revealed no significant difference regarding gender, but significant difference was found regarding locality. Significant positive correlation is found between mental health and teaching effectiveness of college teachers.
Devi & Talukdar (2016)	GALAXY- Int. Interdisciplinary Research Journal	Nalbari District of Assam	The study also attempts to compare the pattern of organizational climate as perceived by male and female college teachers and also try to find out the male and female college teachers perception on organizational climate concerning job satisfaction.	No significant difference of perception of male and female teachers towards organizational climate, significant difference exists between male and female teachers' perception on organizational climate and their job Satisfaction.

Devi & Talukdar (2019)	THINK INDIA (Quarterly Journal)	Kamrup District of Assam	The study is an earnest attempt to recognize the association between teaching effectiveness and attitude towards ICT. It also tried to identify the difference between gender and locality on teaching effectiveness and attitude towards the ICT of college teachers.	The findings covered that there was a significant positive correlation between teaching effectiveness and attitude towards ICT of college teachers. No significant difference in gender on teaching effectiveness and attitude towards ICT. Significant difference in their teaching effectiveness and attitude towards ICT concerning their locality.
Goswami Marami (2007)	Ph.D Thesis, Gauhati University	Kamrup district of Assam	The study examined the relationship between the organizational climate and the academic performance of the students and the relationship between teacher's freezingness and different type's school organizational climate.	The study reveals that the schools of Kamrup District are different in respect to their organizational climate.

Baruah Saswati (2004)	PhD. Thesis. Gauhati University	Kamrup district of Assam	Conducted a study to find out the organizational climate level of government and private school. The study also attempts to investigate any relationship between job satisfaction and organizational climate of High school teachers.	No particular difference was found in organizational climate of government and private schools. Job satisfaction of teachers in schools was positively related with organizational climate of Kamrup district.
Swargiary & Adhikary (2018)	International Journal of Humanities and Social Science Invention	Barpeta District of Assam	An attempt has been made by the investigators to make a comparative study of the school organizational climate of private and government secondary schools of Barpeta District of Assam.	There are variations in the perceptions regarding school organizational climate among the teachers. There exists difference of perceptions between the government and private secondary school teachers.

CHAPTER: 3

METHODOLOGY

"Research is the process of arriving at a dependable solution to the problems through the planned and systematic collection, analysis and interpretation of data"
– Mouley

3.1. Introduction:

Generally, Research methodology is the part that carries the solution of various research problems systematically. It can be regarded as a science because it gives the way of doing research scientifically. Any scientific and psychological research, in particular, requires a systematic scientific application to provide trustworthy information about the proposed goal. Clifford Woody stated that "Research comprises defining and redefining problems, formulating a hypothesis or suggested solutions, collecting, organizing and evaluating data, making deductions and reaching conclusions, carefully testing the conclusions and at last determine whether they fit the formulating hypothesis." Likewise, the present researcher employed a scientific procedure in carrying out the entire study. Research methodology provides a comprehensive representation of the whole research plan of action, followed by the investigators. The research methodology adopted by the investigator based on the aims and hypotheses for the present study is discussed in this chapter.

3.2. Research method:

The research method involves consistent procedure through which the researcher establishes preliminary recognition of the problem to proceed to conclusions. The function of the methodology is to proceed a valid and scientifically approved research work. The methodology comprises of a certain course of action, techniques, and tools for organizing the research work. The excellence of methodology certifies the objective fact of finding which is foremost to bring the consistent conclusions of the research and also the evaluation of the obtained result. Essentially, the procedure is defined as the study of describing, explaining and predicting phenomena by which the work plan of research can be examined. Under it, the researcher familiarizes himself/herself with the various steps generally accepted to study a research problem and accompanying the fundamental logic behind them. Undoubtedly, the methodology is the most important aspect of any study. In the present study, the researcher selected a descriptive survey method as best suitable under investigation.

Hence this section introduces the methodology describing the research design used, the data collection method employed, sampling design, statistical techniques and procedures applied in the analysis. This study used **Quantitative Research Approach**. The reason was that the variables under study were measured quantitatively, such as the psychological scales used to measure teaching effectiveness, organizational climate, mental health and attitude towards ICT scored quantitatively. Again, some other variables, like gender, locality and duration of experience, etc. needed a quantitative approach. Therefore, the researcher argued that the quantitative approach was appropriate for this study. Descriptive methods help in describing, studying and interpreting ''what exists '' regarding variables or requirements in an existing situation. This is concerned with the correlation study that investigates the relationship between variables. For the present study, teaching effectiveness concerning organizational climate, mental health and attitude towards ICT among college teachers; the survey method is best suited.

3.3 Geographical Coverage: Kamrup District (undivided) Assam,

The field of the proposed study is confined to the provincialized college teachers under the affiliation of Gauhati University of Kamrup district, Guwahati, Assam. Here, Kamrup district implies the undivided Kamrup District of Assam which includes Kamrup Rural district and Kamrup Metropolitan district. Initially, Kamrup district was the most densely populated district in entire Assam. On 3rd February 2003, the state government divided the Kamrup district into Kamrup Rural district and Kamrup Metropolitan district. Kamrup (metropolitan) district comprising of the metropolitan city of Guwahati and Kamrup (rural) the rest of the district. For the present study, both Kamrup metropolitan and Kamrup Rural are concerned.

Several related research has been done or is ongoing around the world, with special emphasis on school, secondary and higher secondary level teachers. But there is least related research has done regarding provincialized college teachers in the national and international scenario. Even in Guwahati which is the premier city of North-East India in South-East Asia, little is known about the government college teachers teaching effectiveness, their mental health status, organizational climate setting and also technical knowledge which is predominant for the emerging education system. Therefore, supporting this point the present research was carried out in an unfathomed area in the Indian context and administering the study in Kamrup district, Guwahati may throw some new light on this area of research.

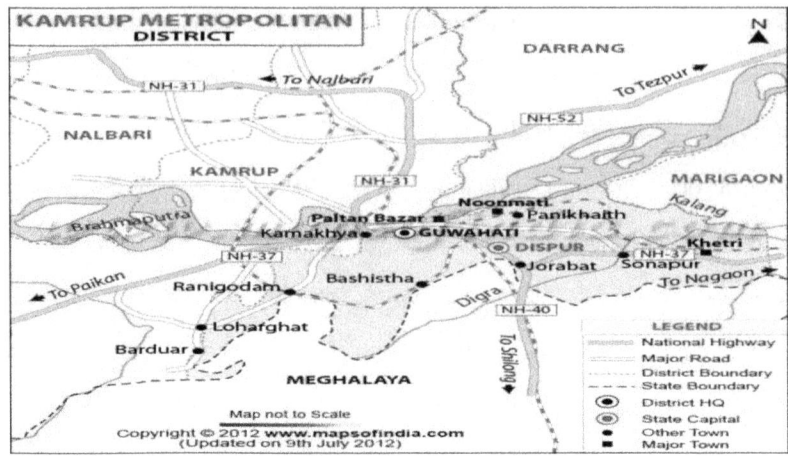

Fig. 3. (i): Map of Kamrup District (Metro)

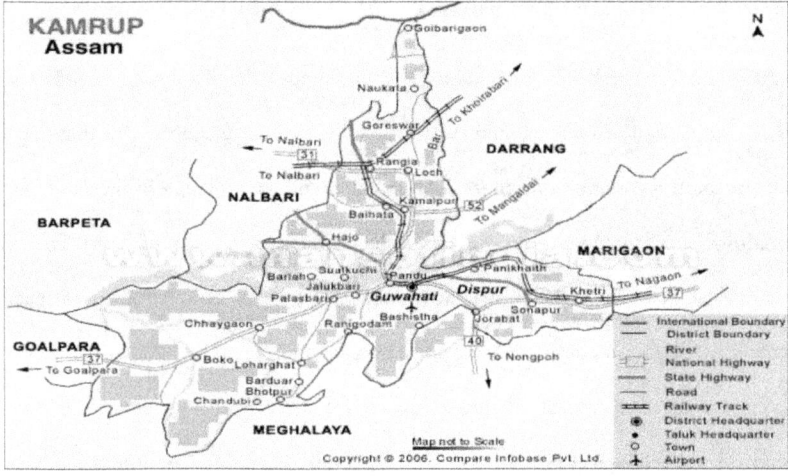

Fig. 3. (ii): Map of Kamrup District (Rural)

This chapter is about the methods employed in carrying out the study and to have a clear and easy understanding. The chapter is divided into four main sections.
These are as follows:
(1) Population &Sample,
(2) Design

(3) Tools,

(4) Procedure

The detail descriptions of the methods employed in the study were enumerated in the following paragraphs.

3.4 Description of population and sample:

3.4.1 Population of the study:

Population of research generally comprises a distinct gathering of ancestor groups or individuals from which a sample is to be formed. Usually, all individuals or objects under a definite population have familiar, required characteristics or traits. However, due to the large size of the population, researchers often cannot test every individual in the population because it is too expensive and time-consuming. Consequently, the researcher has to select a proportionately small quantity or amount of individuals in a systematic order to determine the whole population.

The total population comprises of 914 teachers (according to the data provided by the college authority) from the 14-degree colleges affiliated by Gauhati University of rural and metropolitan areas of Kamrup District, Assam. There are 16 colleges under Gauhati University, but two (2) colleges refused to take part in the survey. So, only 14 colleges are considered for the study. In the existing study, the population pertains to the college teachers working in degree colleges affiliated by Gauhati University of Kamrup District, Assam. The colleges which are located in the Municipality area are considered as urban colleges and the rest of those which are located in the Gaon Panchayat area are considered as rural colleges. The year 2015-2016 has seized as the base year and the population of the study is represented by the Table:

Table 3.1: List of Gauhati University affiliated degree (B.A/B.SC) colleges of Kamrup District, Assam (2015-2016)

Sl. No.	Name of the college	Area of location (Urban/Rural)
1	Arya Vidyapeeth College, Guwahati-16	Urban
2	Dispur College, Dispur-6	Urban
3	Cotton College, Guwahati-1	Urban
4	Handique Girls' College, Guwahati-1	Urban
5	L.C. Bharaliu College, Maligaon, Guwahati-11	Urban
6	Pragjyotish College, Guwahati-9	Urban
7	Pandu College, Guwahati-12	Urban
8	B.P. Chaliha College, Nagarbera-781127	Rural
9	Dakshin Kamrup College, Mirza-781125	Rural
10	North Gauhati College, Guwahati-31	Rural
11	Dimoria College, Khetri- 782403	Rural
12	J.N. College, Boko-781123	Rural
13	Pub-Kamrup College, Baihata Chariali-781381	Rural
14	S.B.M.S. College, Sualkuchi-781103	Rural

(Source: Office of the Registrar, Gauhati University, Guwahati, Assam)

3.4.2 Sample size:

A sample comprises a smaller representative of the whole population which is chosen for extracting information or performing research outcomes for realizing the research objectives. By observing the characteristics of the sample, one can make certain inferences about the characteristics of the population from which it is drawn **(Best & Khan: 2003).**

- The sample of the present research gathered from 14 reputed government colleges under Gauhati University of Kamrup (rural) & Kamrup (metropolitan), Assam participated in the study after gaining consent from the respective colleges. The participation of the subjects was voluntary. The investigator has collected 60% samples out of the total number of population (914) and the total number of samples becomes 548. This is because, at the time of the survey, some teachers were reluctant to participate in the survey process.
- Moreover, those teachers who are not permanent govt. employee under the college and acting as a guest /contractual faculty were also excluded.

Table 3.2: General Allotment of Sample of degree college teachers

Occupation	Age range (years)	Duration of Experience	Sample
College Teachers (Urban)	24-35　36-46　47-57	1-10 years　11-20 years　Above 21 years	137 Male　137 Female
College Teachers (Rural)	24-35　36-46　47-57	1-10 years　11-20 years　Above 21 years	137 Male　137 Female
		Total Sample	548

Distribution of the samples according to the three variables viz, gender, locality & duration of experience.

Table 3.3: Distribution of samples based on gender

Gender	Number	%
Male	274	50
Female	274	50
Total	548	100

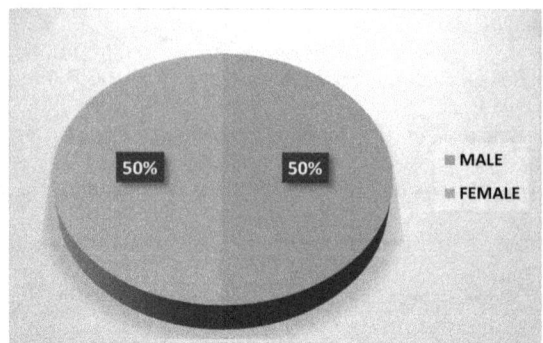

Fig.3.3: Pie diagram showing the % distribution of samples based on gender

Table 3.4: Distribution of samples based on locality

Locality	No	%
Rural	274	50
Urban	274	50
Total	548	100

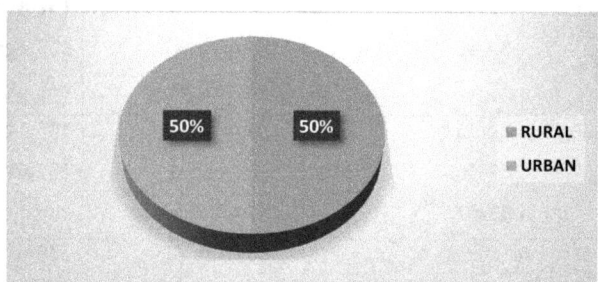

Fig.3.4: Pie diagram showing the % distribution of samples based on locality

Table 3.5: Distribution of samples based on duration of experience

Duration of experience	No	%
1-10 years	153	27.91
11-20 years	223	40.69
Above 20 years	172	31.38
Total	548	100

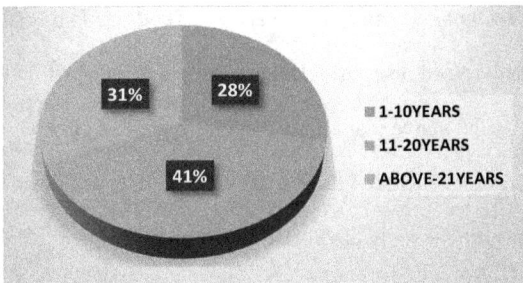

Fig.3.5: Pie diagram showing the % distribution of samples based on experience

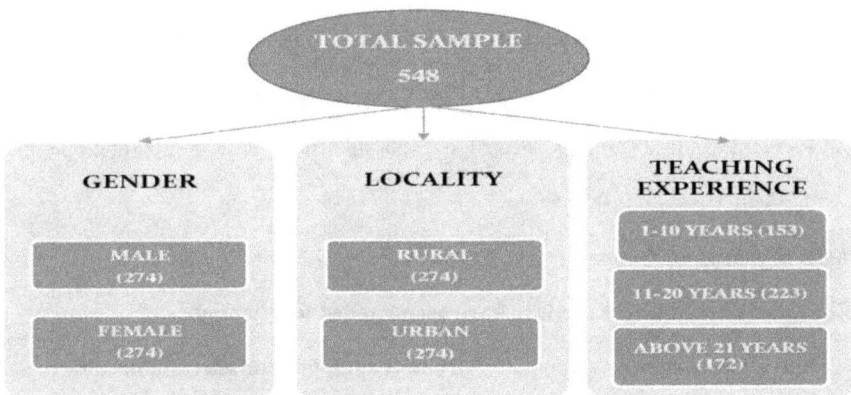

Fig.3.6: Distribution of sample for the study

3.4.2. A) Criteria for selection of sample:

Following criteria has been taken for inclusion of a student in the sample:

- He/she should be a permanent teacher in the provincialized degree college.
- He/she should be working in provincialized degree colleges located in Kamrup (rural) & Kamrup (metropolitan) district, Assam.
- He/she should be within the teaching experience of 1-10, 11-20 and above 21 years.
- Both male and female participants should be included in the survey.
- College teachers whose chronological age ranged from 24-57 years.

103

3.4.2. B) Source of data and criteria for selection of college: In this study for obtaining the data, four standardized psychological scales are conducted united with all the samples. As it has stated above that all the samples comprise of college teachers so, the source of collecting data includes the establishment of educational phenomena. The inclusion of colleges for the study is selected based on the following criteria:

> ➤ Provincialized degree colleges which offer both B.A. and B.Sc. courses are selected. From the collected list of affiliated colleges, it is found that the number of provincialized degree colleges offering only B.A. course is very less.
> ➤ Colleges affiliated to Gauhati University only are selected.
> ➤ Provincialized colleges located in Kamrup (rural) & Kamrup (metropolitan) district, Assam is selected.

3.4.2. C) Sampling Technique:

Two types of sampling procedure have been applied for the study:

1. Multi-stage sampling technique: Purposive sampling for selecting the degree Colleges

2. Proportionate stratified random sampling technique: for selecting the college teachers

For selecting the number of colleges of the present study **purposive sampling** has been applied and fourteen (14) degree colleges (comprising B.A/B.SC courses) have been selected. Out of fourteen-degree colleges seven (7) colleges are located in urban areas and the other seven (7) colleges are located in rural areas. The **proportionate stratified random sampling technique** has been employed to take the sample of the study. After determining the sample, teachers working in degree colleges are classified into different strata to meet the objectives like location, gender, and teaching experience. The first classification is based on the location of the college and divided into two groups namely urban and rural. Second, the investigator has divided the whole sample into two strata based on gender i.e. male/female. Lastly, the investigator has divided the sample into another stratum based on teaching experience i.e. 1-10 years/11-20 years/above 21 years of experience.

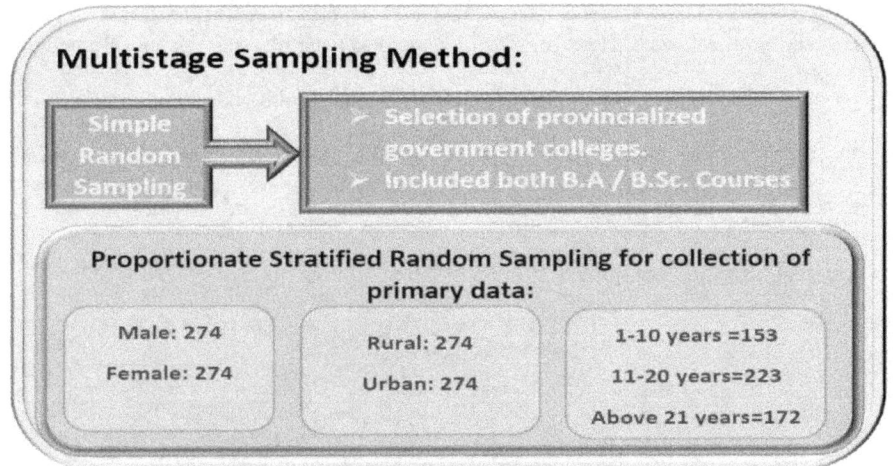

Fig.3.7:Multi-stage sampling method

3.5 Research design:

Research design may be referred to as the plan, structure, and strategy of investigation conceived to obtain answers to research questions and control variances (**Kerlinger, 1973**). Research design is the preliminary draft of the comprehensive approaches to proving the hypothesis and analysing the obtained data. It enables the researchers to make a logical and precise goal-oriented answer regarding the stated research problem. A research design is defined as the sequential forms for accumulation and analysis of data in a systematic way that aims to incorporate relevant information to the research purpose. Indeed, it is the conceptual structure within which research is conducted.

In this study, **quantitative research methods** are utilized to test the proposed hypotheses. The **descriptive method of research** is employed for the present study as the method is concerned with surveying, describing and investigating the existing phenomenon, conditions and relationship that exists. Descriptive research also referred to as survey research **(Gay & Airasian, 2000)** is mainly concerned with "attitudes, opinions, preferences, demographics, practices, and procedures." The present study is **correlational research**. Here, an effort is mould to determine the relationship between teaching effectiveness, organizational climate, mental health and attitude towards ICT for gender (male and female); type of locality (rural and urban); and teaching experience status of college teachers (**1-10** years, **11-20** years and above **21** years).

3.6 Variable under study:

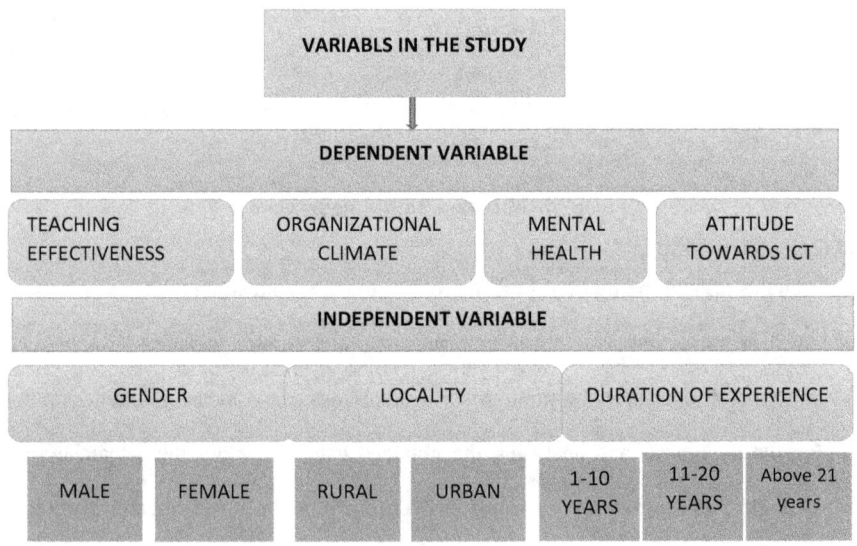

Fig.3.8: Variable for the study

3.7: Data collection:

3.7.1. The procedure of primary data collection:

It is an accepted fact that in any kind of research work, the procedure of collecting the data is regarded as one of the important phenomena. The primary data for the present study were collected between the periods **September 2015 to February 2016** in the study area of fieldwork is Kamrup district. During the data collection following steps are maintained-

Step 1: At the inceptive stage of the study, the investigator taken the list of Gauhati University affiliated degree colleges from the office of the registrar of Gauhati University. After completing the selection process of B.A/ B.SC colleges, the researcher initiated to visit the colleges' doorstep. Then the investigator visited personally every selected college and met the principal and clarified the purpose of the visit.

Step 2: After getting permission, the investigator visited the institution and met teachers in the department wise and explained the purpose of the study. They are also asked to convey that they will be given a few psychological questionnaires to be filled up which needs to be undertaken for research purposes. They were also asked to take part voluntarily and consents are obtained without any force. The participants are also informed that the information they provided would be kept confidential as it only would be applied only for research purposes. After that, the administration procedures of the tools were started.

Step 3: Then, the investigator distributed all the four questionnaires among the participants and asked to fill up all the questions without leaving any items unanswered. The subjects were told that there was no time limit for the completion of the scale, but they could complete the entire scale in a short period. At, first, the personal information datasheet is filled up by the investigator within 5 to 10 minutes. After that the Teacher Effectiveness Scale (consisting of 68 items), Employees Mental Health Inventory (comprising 24 items), Self-devised College Climate Questionnaire (28 items) and also Attitude towards Information Technology for College Teachers (23 items) developed by the researcher was distributed among the teachers one by one. Instructions included all questionnaires were read out to the teachers, and doubts regarding any statements also cleared on the spot. The participants were also requested to give a response to every question with honesty and sincere effort. Thus, the data collection procedures were completed under this condition. The teachers had given their response and they took a short period to complete the administration of the test. After completion of the test, the questionnaires were collected and the participants were offered thanks for their kind cooperation in the survey. In the end, all concerned principals, the authority, Head of the Departments (HOD) were ended with a vote of thanks for giving consent for the collection of data. Later, the score of each questionnaire provided by the participants was analysed and calculated with the help of requisite statistical analysis. After collecting data, the score of the answer sheets was done strictly according to the directions of the manual and then analysed statistically.

3.7.2. Secondary data collection:

Firstly the researcher gathered the secondary data from diverse sources to gain prevailing information on the subject-matter of the study. As the secondary source of different books, National and International Research Journals, PhD Thesis, M. Phil. Dissertations, encyclopaedia, Websites, papers had been used to collect necessary information for the study. To collect the secondary sources of data the investigator had visited different libraries and institutions which are given below:

1. K.K Handique Library, Gauhati University, Assam
2. Department of Library, Documentation, and Information, N.C.E.R.T., Sri Aurobindo Marg, New Delhi
3. Dibrugarh University Library, Dibrugarh, Assam
4. Omeo Kumar Das Institute of Social Change and Development, Guwahati, Assam
5. North-Eastern Hill University Central Library, Shillong, Meghalaya
6. State Central Library, Guwahati, Assam
7. Libraries of some Provincialized Colleges of Assam

3.8: Description of the tools:

In conducting research, an investigator needs to utilize some devices or instruments to gather or to explore facts from the pertinent fields. These acts of data collecting appliances are called a research tool. The appropriateness of any research accomplishment particularly depends upon the research tool. So, there is a necessity for an appropriate selection of the tools by the investigator. The main considerable relevance of research tools entails its usefulness, consistency and validity means genuineness or purposefulness. For above-mentioned prerequisite of effective research tools and the analysis of teaching effectiveness, organizational climate, mental health and attitude towards ICT following research tools were employed by the investigator.

Table 3.6: Research tools used

Sl. No.	Variables	Tools	Prepared by
3.6.1	Teaching Effectiveness	Teacher Effectiveness Scale	Dr. Shallu Puri & Prof. S.C. Gakhar
3.6.2	Organizational Climate	Self-devised questionnaire	Trishna Devi & Dr. Mala Chaliha Talukdar

3.6.3	Mental Health	Employee's Mental Health Inventory	Dr. Jagdish
3.6.4	Attitude towards ICT	Self-devised questionnaire	Trishna Devi & Dr. Mala Chaliha Talukdar

3.8.1. *Teacher Effectiveness Scale (TES):*

Teacher Effectiveness Scale (in short known as TES) was furnished and designed by Shallu Puri & S.C. Gakhar of the department of Education of Punjab University, in Chandigarh. This scale was published by Manasvi Publication situated in UG-1, Nirmal Height, Mathura Road, Agra-282007. The scale consisted of 68 items based on six dimensions. The scale is designed to study the effectiveness of teachers teaching at the college level, postgraduate level or also senior secondary classes. The dimensions and item-wise serial no. are given in the following categories-

Table 3.7: Categories of TES along with the items

Sl. No.	Category	Item wise Serial No.	Total
I	Academic & professional knowledge	1,2,3,4,5	05
II	Preparation & presentation of lesson plan, classroom management	17,30,31,34,39,40,41,42,43,44,45, 47,48,49,50,51,60 ,65	18
III	Attitude towards students/ head of institution/ colleagues/parents,	6,7,12,13,14,15,16,18,19,20,23, 26,27,28,63,64	16
IV	Use of motivation reward/ punishment/interest in all round development of students	8,9,10,11,36,37,38	07
V	Result, feedback accountability	61,62,48,66,67,68	06
VI	Personal qualities	21,22,24,25,29,32,33,46, 52,53,54,55,57,58,59	16
	Total		68

Administration and scoring: The scale is designed for the teacher educators to measure the effectiveness at different levels. Preferably, 68 statements are included based on the expert's opinion and argument. The investigator decided to use Thurston's five-point technique scale and the teacher educators explained the statements by giving their agreement or disagreement. Respondents rate statements using a six-point format: strongly agree-(5), agree-(4), undecided-(3), disagree-(2), strongly disagree-(1). The maximum score ranges as 340 and the minimum score will be 68. The high scores indicate high effectiveness on the dimension assessed. The limitation of filling the questionnaire is 40 minutes. The total raw scores for the whole test is interpreted based on the effectiveness level given below:

Table 3.8: Level of teacher effectiveness

Raw Scores	Level
301-340	Very High
270-299	High
200-269	Average
--------	Low
--------	Very Low

Level of teaching effectiveness is interpreted according to the response values of the respondents. The TES questionnaire contains 68 items. It is a Likert scale i.e. each question has five (5) possible responses from strongly agree to strongly disagree having weightage five (5) to one (1). Suppose, one respondent has given strongly agree responses to all the 68 items, then the highest raw score will be 340. Again, another respondent has given minimum score one (1) to all 68 items, then the score will be 68. So, in such a way we have raw score range from 68-340.

Table 3.9: Reliability of teacher effectiveness

Reliability Co-efficient (Gutman Split-Half, Number of items- 68)	Spearman-Brown Co-efficient	Cronbach's Alpha
.926	.927	.964

Validity: The scale was justified against the criterion of "Content Validity". Content validity means the acceptability of sampling of a specified universe of content. For determining content validity the scale items along with the outcomes were given to the panel which consists of seven experts. Based on the assignment of scale items the experts agreed 92% validity of the items with the investigator.

3.8.2. *Organizational Climate Questionnaire*: The organizational climate questionnaire is self-devised. The following steps are followed by the researcher to construct a questionnaire for the research work.

(a) **Collection and writing of items**: In the beginning, suggestions for the construction and development of the questionnaire were received from the principals, educationists, and members associated with the organization. Following the ideas suggested by them, the investigator was made a list of questions related to the perception of organizational climate of colleges. The number of questions was 42. After discussion with the educationist these 42 statements were then categorized in terms of the several dimensions of organizational climate as given below:

(i) Physical Environment
(ii) Library Facilities
(iii) Reward System of the organization
(iv) Relationship with colleagues
(v) Support System
(vi) Academic Climate

Thus, the blueprint of 42 items was produced to identify the organizational climate. Additionally, the statement or item was also established. The items included in the draft were of multiple options having five alternatives. To make the testing more reliable negative statements were also included.

Scrutiny and critique: After fulfilment of the first draft of the scale, a pilot study was undertaken on a sample of 80 college teachers from three colleges of Kamrup district. Then, the researcher performed the study providing the questionnaire of 42 statements related to different fields to college teachers. The teachers were also requested to give their analytical responses regarding the language, meaningfulness, and expansion of statements related to organizational climate.

As a result of the expert opinions, few statements were improved. Suggestions were discussed and incorporated in the draft by improving all the mistakes. The revised version of the scale, consisting of 35 rating type items measuring the perception of organizational climate approved by the experts.

(c) Final Draft of organizational climate questionnaire: The following table gives us an idea of the organizational climate scale and its contents in its final form:

Table 3.10: Organizational climate questionnaire in final form

Sl. No	Dimensions		Serial wise item number	Total	Total items
1	Physical Environment	Positive	1, 3, 4, 6	4	7
		Negative	2,5,7	3	
2	Library Facilities	Positive	8,10,11	3	5
		Negative	9,12	2	
3	Reward System of the Organization	Positive	13,15,16	3	5
		Negative	14,17	2	
4	Relationship with	Positive	18,21	2	4

		Negative	19,20	2	
5	Support system	Positive	22,23,25,27	4	6
		Negative	24,26	2	
6	Academic Climate	Positive	28,29,31,34,35	5	8
		Negative	30,32,33	3	
				Total	35

d) Administration of the scale:

The Organizational Climate questionnaire a self-reporting scale was administered on 548 subjects included teachers from provincialized degree colleges from both rural and urban areas. The purpose of the scale was clearly explained to the subjects and it also assured that their replies would be kept confidential. It was also emphasized that items should not be excluded as there were no right or wrong responses. There was no time limit for completing the questionnaire. Thus participants were provided with complete and accurate procedural information to fill up the questionnaire.

e) Scoring:

Table 3.11: Scoring of organizational climate questionnaire

Sl. No	Type of statements	Strongly Agree	Agree	Undecided	Disagree	Strongly Disagree
1	Positive	5	4	3	2	1
2	Negative	1	2	3	4	5

The polarity of the negative items in the Likert-type scale was reversed.

Table 3.12: Level of organizational climate

Raw Scores	Level
109-122	Highly favorable climate
95-108	Positive favorable climate
85-94	Moderate favorable climate
71-84	Unfavorable climate
64-69	Highly unfavorable climate

f) **Reliability and Validity:** The reliability of this study is tested through Cronbach's alpha and Guttman Split-Half coefficient. The reliability coefficient value is given in a tabular form.

Table 3.13: Reliability analysis of organizational climate questionnaire

Reliability Co-efficient (Gutman Split-Half, Number of items- 68)	Spearman-Brown Co-efficient	Cronbach's Alpha
.718	.816	.747

The questionnaire has fairly high face validity. Content validity for the statements was also confirmed by the expertise. The questionnaire was assessed at the time of conduction and after the development of the items. Feedback from the panel of professionals was taken to make revisions and clarity of the questionnaire. After close analysis items for which there has been 100% agreement amongst judges regarding their relevance to organizational climate are included in the questionnaire.

3.8.3. *Employee's Mental Health Inventory*: It was developed by Jagdish, Department of Psychology, R.B.S. College, Agra. The inventory is 24-items scale designed to assess the mental health of employees working in any organization. The belief is that this inventory may be useful in screening the employees with poor psychological well-being who need help to their happier job and personal life.

Development of the inventory: The investigator set 60 small and easy items to measure the mental health of the employee and against each item for response 'Yes' and 'No' alternatives were written. Then the items were presented before 10 experts with a request to give their opinions regarding the relevance of the items. The items commonly approved by the experts were retained in the test. Then the revised items were administered to 30 employees working in an organization. They were asked to give comments and suggestions on wordings of items and difficulty in answering. Some items were revised in the light of the suggestions mentioned by the respondents. Thus, out of 60 items, 45 were retained for item analysis.

Item Analysis: The preliminary form of the EMHI consisting of 45 items was conducted to a sample of 200 individuals working in different organizations. The scores obtained by the subjects were tabulated and analysis of item was carried out to identify the discriminatory power of the items of the test. The extreme group technique was adopted for item analysis. The items revealing significant differences were retained for the final form of the test. Thus, 24 items indicating significant discriminative power were taken for the concluding form of the inventory.

Scoring: The inventory has both positive and negative statements. The responses indicating 'yes' alternatives about positive (indicative of good mental health) items are to be awarded a score of one and 'No' alternatives are to be awarded a score of zero. The scoring would be reverse for negatively worded items.

Table 3.14: Scoring of EMHI

Items	Responses	Score
Positive items (4,14,18,22)	'Yes' marked	1
	'No' marked	0
Negative items (Except the above items)	'Yes' marked	0
	'No' marked	1

Table 3.15: Level of interpretation of EMHI

Raw scores	Level of interpretation
23 and Above	Very high
22	High
16-21	Medium
13-15	Low
12 and Below	Very low

Reliability: The split-half reliability of the test was decided by computing the Pearson Product Moment coefficient of correlation between odd-even halves of the inventory. The obtained reliability coefficient, corrected with the Spearman-Brown Prophecy formula.

Table 3.16: Reliability of the Inventory (EMHI)

Reliability Co-efficient (Gutman Split-Half, Number of items- 68)	Spearman-Brown Co-efficient	Cronbach's Alpha
.642	.701	.779

Validity: Construct validity is determined by computing the coefficient of correlation between the scores on the EMHI and Mental Health Scale (Buck, 1972). The coefficient found to be .74.

3.8.4. Attitude towards ICT: The attitude towards ICT questionnaire is self-devised. To construct a questionnaire for the research work the following steps are followed.

The first draft of the questionnaire: Initially the Attitude towards ICT questionnaire consisted of 40 statements selected based on previous studies and discussion with 10 experts working in degree colleges of Kamrup district. After discussion with the experts these 40 statements were then categorized in terms of the several dimensions of organizational climate as given below:

a) Productivity of teaching
b) Usefulness for students
c) Teachers interest and acceptance

After that, the form of the statement or item was also established which contained multiple- choice type having five alternatives. To make the testing more valid negative statements were also included.

After accomplishment of the first design of the questionnaire, a pilot study was done on a sample of 50 college teachers from three-degree colleges of Kamrup district. The researcher has visited each college to take permissions from the authority before conducting the survey. After that, the researcher investigated the study providing the questionnaire of 40 statements related to different fields of college teachers. The teachers were also requested to give suggestions regarding the wordings, meaningfulness, and expansion of statements related to attitude towards ICT.

As a result of the difficulties mentioned by the respondents, some of the items were modified. The revised version of the scale, consisting of 23 rating type items held on for construction. And then a final form of a questionnaire was made.

Table 3.17: Attitude towards ICT questionnaire in final form

Sl. No	Dimensions		Serial wise item number	Total	Total items
1	Productivity of teaching	Positive	1,2,4,6		7
		Negative	3,5,7		
2	Usefulness for students	Positive	8,10,11,13,14		7
		Negative	9,12		
3	Teachers interest and acceptance	Positive	16,17,19,21,23		10
		Negative	15,18,20,22		
				Total	24

Scoring: The questionnaire has both positive and negative statements. The contradiction of the negative items on the Likert-type scale was reversed.

Table 3.18: scoring for Attitude towards ICT questionnaire

Sl. No	Type of statements	Strongly Agree	Agree	Undecided	Disagree	Strongly Disagree
1	Positive	5	4	3	2	1
2	Negative	1	2	3	4	5

Table 3.19: Level of interpretation of Attitude towards ICT

Raw scores	Level of interpretation
96-109	Highly favorable attitude
83-95	Positive favorable attitude
74-82	Moderate favorable attitude
61-73	Unfavorable attitude
23-60	Highly unfavorable attitude

Reliability and Validity: The reliability of this study determined by Cronbach's alpha and Guttman Split-Half coefficient. The reliability coefficient value is mentioned below:

Table 3.20: Reliability of Attitude towards ICT questionnaire

Reliability Co-efficient (Gutman Split-Half, Number of items- 24)	Spearman-Brown Co-efficient	Cronbach's Alpha
.701	.706	.745

Validity: The scale was validated against the criterion of "Content Validity" established by the experts. For establishing validity, feedback from the experts was used as before and after the conduction of the pilot study. Based on the analysis of the scale items the experts agreed 100% reading their relevance to attitude towards ICT is enclosed with the questionnaire.

3.9 Statistical techniques used for the present study:

Based on the objectives of the study, and account of the administrations of tools, the collected data were analysed through appropriate statistical techniques. For quantities analysis, the various statistical techniques were applied. Both inferential and descriptive statistics have been utilized for analysis. The data which is collected through the questionnaire had been systematically arranged and sorted based on their characteristics. Through the tabulation procedure, the investigator tries to make the data systematic and easily understandable.

To make the data easily understandable table, Pie diagram and graphical representation are also done. A Bar diagram had been used here to represent the data.

Descriptive statistics:

(I) The simple percentages had been calculated to observe the teaching effectiveness, organizational climate, mental health and attitude towards ICT of the degree college teachers.

(II) The measure of central tendency: - Mean, Median and Mode were calculated for further calculation of the data.

(III) The measure of variability: Standard Deviation was also calculated to study the variation of the score.

(IV) Descriptive 'z' score was calculated to find the significance of mean differences in categories of teaching effectiveness, organizational climate, mental health and attitude towards ICT of the degree college teachers based on gender (male/female); locality (rural/urban); duration of experience (1-10 years, 11-20 years and above 21 years).

Inferential Statistics:

- The statistical test ANOVA was applied to find out a difference in groups of college teachers based on the duration of experience, followed by Tuckey's Test.
- Pearson product-moment correlation was used to determine the relationship between teaching effectiveness, organizational climate, mental health and attitude towards ICT (along with its dimensions).
- Multiple regression analysis was performed to test the contribution of organizational climate, mental health, and attitude towards ICT in predicting teaching effectiveness among college teachers.

3.10 Ethical issues considered:

The following steps were taken for ensuring quality data:

- Permission was taken from the principal of the Institute for data collection.
- It was told to the participants that the activities undertaken were for research purposes.
- Voluntary participation was obtained from all the participants and no one was enforced to participate in the study.
- The confidentiality of information was ensured.
- The participants were told that they could withdraw from the study at any time without any obligation, even after giving consent, if they wished so.
- In any psychological research debriefing is an important procedure which involves the detail discussion of the study within the researcher and the participants after an experiment or study has been concluded. It can be assumed as a structured or semi-structured interview approach.

- So, after the completion of the questionnaires, the participants were provided with accurate and appropriate information about the essence and purpose of the study. In this process, the participants were also allowed to ask any queries relevant to the research practices.

CHAPTER: 4
RESULT, ANALYSIS AND DISCUSSION

4.1 INTRODUCTION:

Analysis and interpretation of the data is essentially a useful and utility-based research activity, which is frequently described as the "core of the Research". The process of interpretation is essentially explained what the result has been observed, what they mean and what is their significance. So, interpretation is not only a careful and significant study but also a logical, theoretical and critical conception of the result obtained after analysis. In this chapter, the investigator has tried to accomplish the objectives of the study by analysing the data with the application of selected statistical techniques. The purpose of the data analysis is to reduce data into an intelligible and simpler form so that the relations of research problems can be easily found out and interpreted. After the analysis of data, it is the essential task on the part of the researchers to draw inferences or conclusions which help the investigator to interpret without misleading information.

This chapter presents the analysis and interpretation of data and the research findings which reveal the acceptance and rejection of the hypothesis. In the present study, data have been analysed by using simple percentages, Mean, S.**D**., 'Z' test, **ANOVA** or F-test, Pearson co-efficient of correlation 'r' and multiple regression analysis to test of significance of data. After scoring the raw score, obtained data were entered into SPSS software package for further analysis. The analysis and interpretation of data based on objectives and related hypothesis have been presented in this chapter objective wise.

4.2 STATISTICAL ANALYSIS:

Objective No. 1: To compare the teaching effectiveness of male and female college teachers.

(Ho1) There will be no significant difference in teaching effectiveness of male and female college teachers.

Table 4.1 (A): Level of teaching effectiveness on the basis of gender

TES Groups	Gender					
	Male		Female		Total	
	Count	%	Count	%	Count	%
Very low	0	.0	0	.0	0	.0
Low	0	.0	0	.0	0	.0
Average	119	43.4	127	46.7	246	45.0
High	91	33.1	72	26.5	163	29.8
Very high	64	23.5	73	26.8	137	25.2
Total	274	100	274	100	548	100.0

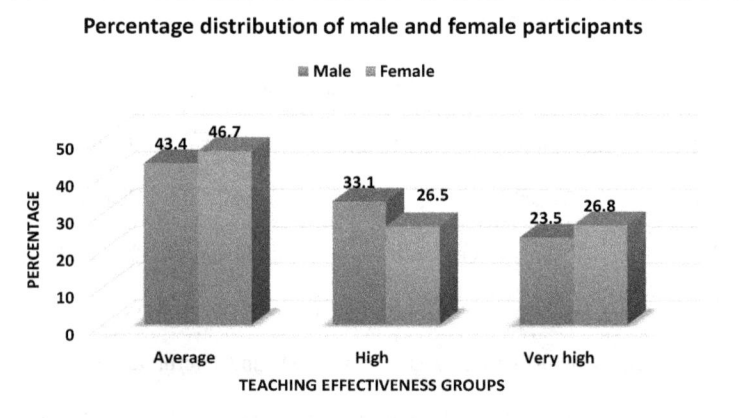

Fig.4.1 (A): Percentage distribution of teaching effectiveness on the basis of gender

Table4.1. (A) Shows that 43.4 % of male college teachers have an average level of teaching effectiveness, 33.1% have high, 23.5% have a very high level and no male teachers have a low and very low level of teaching effectiveness. As well, 46.7% of female college teachers have an average level of teaching effectiveness, 26.5% have a high, 26.8% have a very high level and no female teachers have a low and very low level of effectiveness. This means that both genders have a satisfactory level of teaching effectiveness.

Table 4.1 (B): Comparison of teaching effectiveness based on gender

TES Dimensions	Male		Female			
	Mean	SD	Mean	SD	Z	P-value
1) Academic and professional knowledge	20.6	2.73	20.7	2.55	-.717	.473
2) Preparation and presentation of lesson plan, classroom management	100.7	11.07	101.8	11.41	-.894	.371
3) Attitude towards students, parents, colleagues, head of institution	63.2	6.68	63.5	6.34	-.120	.905
4) Use of motivation, reward and punishment and interest in all round development of students	29.0	3.77	28.8	3.77	-.616	.538
5) Result, feedback accountability	7.3	1.58	7.5	1.44	-.720	.471
6) Personal qualities	57.2	6.08	57.6	6.32	-.359	.720
Total	278.0	27.89	279.9	28.57	-.589	.556

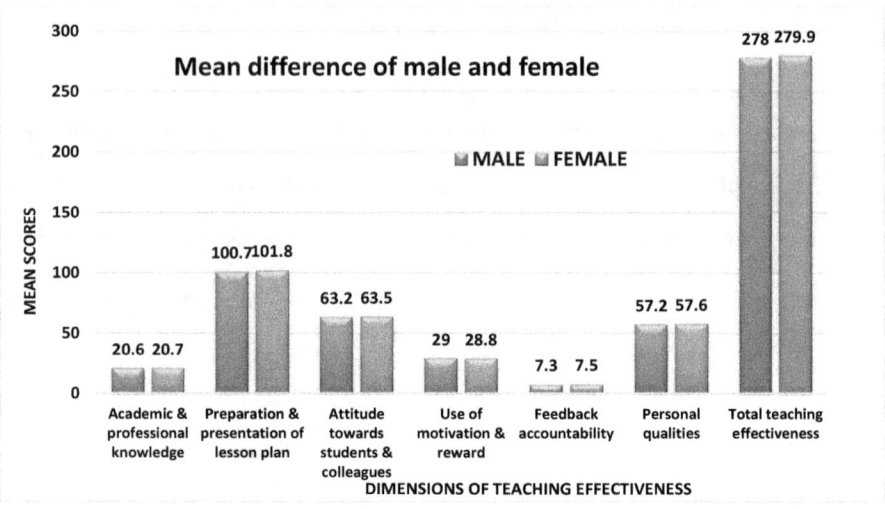

Fig.4.1 (B): Graphical representation of teaching effectiveness based on gender

Interpretation:

Data from **Table4**.1 **(B)** shows that the 'Z' value at P<0.05 in terms of teaching effectiveness is not found to be statistically significant for male and female college teachers. Thus, the first hypothesis **(Ho1)** is accepted. The total mean score of male and female participants lies in **278** and **279.9** accordingly which indicates a high level of effectiveness **(as mentioned in table 3.8)**. Based on the obtained mean score, it can be said that the teaching effectiveness on different areas of female teachers is better than the male teachers. Moreover, there is a perception that the status of women is higher in the North Eastern Region of the country in comparison with the status of women in all India average **(Rustagi, 2004)**. But the overall result indicates that both male and female teachers have almost the same level of competency.

This finding that reveals no gender difference in teaching effectiveness may be because both of them are more accountable to cooperative classroom teaching, well acquainted with the teaching objectives, and above all, they are provided equal opportunities for proper development with real-life situations. It is agreeable that classroom management has been determined as the highest efficacy dimension for all the teachers. As the obtained results reveal no gender difference in the effectiveness of teachings because both of them are compatible with formulating course design, interpersonal relations, learning assessment, and efficient in technical knowledge. This finding is also in conformity with the earlier studies conducted by **Kumari & Padhi (2014)**; **Rani & Devi (2015)**; **Seema (2015)**; **Dash & Barman (2016)**; **Kumar (2016)** has examined the teaching effectiveness of higher secondary school teachers and did not find a significant difference between male and female college teachers. Similarly, a study conducted in secondary and higher secondary school teachers by **Pachaiyappan and Raj (2014)** indicated gender did not influence the potency of teachers. Another study conducted by **Arya & Singh (2016)** reveals no significant difference in teacher's effectiveness among senior secondary and secondary level school.

Objective No. 2: To compare the level of teaching effectiveness of rural and urban college teachers.

(Ho2) There will be no significant difference of locality (rural/urban) on teaching effectiveness of college teachers.

Table 4.2 (A): Level of teaching effectiveness on the basis of locality

TES Groups	Locality					
	Rural		Urban		Total	
	Count	%	Count	%	Count	%
Very low	0	.0	0	.0	0	.0
Low	0	.0	0	.0	0	.0
Average	169	62.1	77	27.9	246	45.0
High	73	26.5	90	33.1	163	29.8
Very high	32	11.4	107	39.0	139	25.2
Total	274	100	274	100	548	100.0

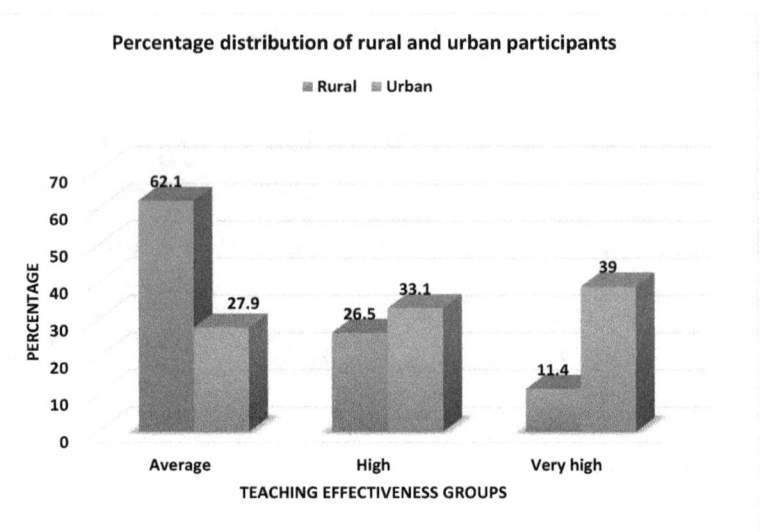

Fig.4.2 (A): **Percentage distribution of teaching effectiveness on the basis of locality**

Table4.2 (A) shows that **62.**1% of rural college teachers have an average level of effectiveness, **26.**5% have high, 11.4% have very high and no rural college teachers have a low, very low level of effectiveness. In an urban area, college teachers with 27.9% have an average level of effectiveness, 33.1% have a high level, and 39.0% have very high and no urban college teachers have a low and very low level of teaching effectiveness. This means that in rural areas maximum percentage lies in average groups which postulate that rural college teachers foster an average level of effectiveness. College teachers combining with urban areas show the optimal percentage in high and very high groups. So, it displays that teachers in urban areas have shown higher teaching effectiveness.

Table 4.2 (B): Comparison of teaching effectiveness on the basis of locality

TES dimension	Rural		Urban		Sig
	Mean	SD	Mean	SD	
1. Academic and professional knowledge	20.0	2.56	21.3	2.55	.000**
2. Preparation and presentation of lesson plan, classroom management	97.7	9.69	104.9	11.53	.000**
3. Attitude towards students, parents, colleagues, head of institution	61.3	6.19	65.5	6.15	.000**
4. Use of motivation, reward and punishment and interest in all round development of students	27.7	3.75	30.0	3.45	.000**
5. Result, feedback accountability	7.0	1.42	7.8	1.49	.000**
6. Personal qualities	55.0	5.17	59.8	6.23	.000**
TES_TOTAL	268.7	24.45	289.3	28.01	.000**

**Significant level is at P<0.01

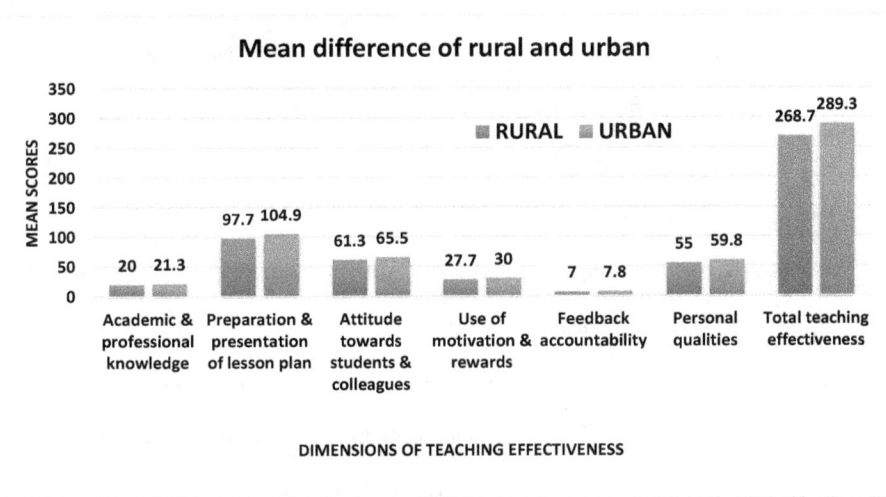

Fig.4.2 (B): Graphical representation of teaching effectiveness based on locality

Interpretation:

Data from **Table 4.2 (B)** shows highly significant difference in terms of teaching effectiveness between rural and urban college teachers. Therefore, the hypothesis **(Ho2)** is rejected.

The "Z" value was found to be statistically significant at $P<0.01$ in different dimensions of teaching effectiveness between rural and urban college teachers. It means that the locality of college has a significant influence on teaching effectiveness. Based on the obtained mean score, urban college teachers' teaching effectiveness **(289.3)** also found at a high level **(as mentioned in table 3.8)** that is comparatively better than the rural college teachers **(268.7)** which lies in the average level of effectiveness. Moreover, urban teachers scored higher on the preparation and presentation of lesson plan classroom management techniques, providing interest in the all-round development of the students, and enhancement of personal qualities of teachers than that of rural teachers. That is because the rural college teachers may have a lack of adequate classroom environment, teacher's involvement, interpersonal relationships, student's responses, and difficulty in using proper teaching methods which affect the effectiveness of teachers.

Previous research also supports the present findings. **Pachaiyappan and Raj (2014)** indicated similar results where Secondary and Higher Secondary School teachers from urban areas hold an upper hand as compared to those of rural areas. A study conducted by **Kumar and Kaur (2017)** found a significant difference between localities regarding their effectiveness of engineering college teachers in teaching. Again, the findings of the present study corroborate with the earlier findings **Malik & Sharma (2013)** who reported that Secondary School Teachers in remote areas feel more professional hindrance as compare to urban areas. Further, **Thirumavalavan & Balakrishnan (2013)** inferred in their study that urban teacher education colleges implied a greater level of effectiveness in comparison to rural areas.

Objective No.3: To compare the level of teaching effectiveness based on the duration of experience (1-10, 11-20, 21 and above years).

(Ho3) There will be no significant difference in duration of experience on teaching effectiveness of college teachers.

Table 4.3(A): Level of teaching effectiveness on the basis of teaching experience

TES Groups	Teaching experience							
	1-10 Years		11-20 Years		Above 21 Years		Total	
	Count	%	Count	%	Count	%	Count	%
Very low	0	.0	0	.0	0	.0	0	.0
Low	0	.0	0	.0	0	.0	0	.0
Average	46	29.8	74	33.2	87	51.2	245	45.0
High	59	39.1	99	44.4	45	25.3	162	29.8
Very high	48	31.1	50	22.4	40	23.5	137	25.2
Total	153	100.0	223	100.0	172	100.0	548	100.0

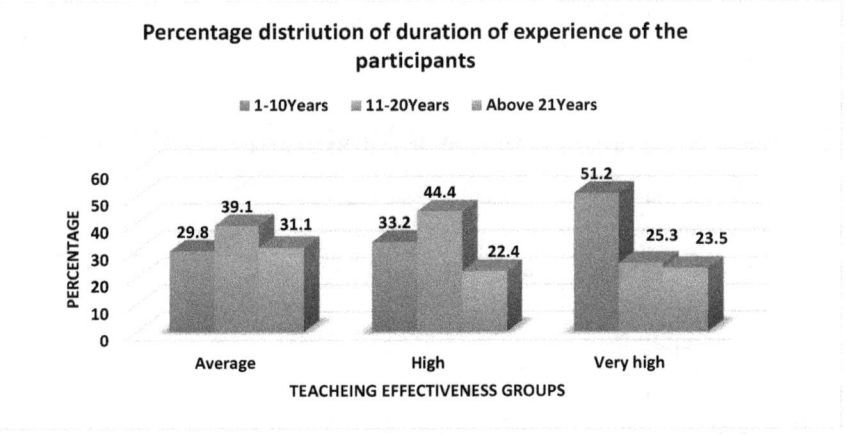

Fig.4.3 (A): Percentage distribution of teaching effectiveness based on experience

Table 4.3 (A) shows that 29.8% of teachers with 1-10 years of teaching experience have an average level of effectiveness, 39.1% have high, 31.1% have very high and no teachers perceive a low and very low level of effectiveness. Again, 33.2% with 11-20 years have an average level of effectiveness, 44.4% have a high level, 22.4% have a very high level and no college teachers have faced a low and very low level of effectiveness. Hence, 51.2% with above 21 years have an average level of effectiveness, 25.3% have a high level, 23.5% have to exploit a very high level and no college teachers have a low and very low level of effectiveness. This means that teachers with 1-10, 11-20 years experience can perceive a high level of effectiveness while in above 21 years teachers find out with an average level of teaching effectiveness.

Table4.3 (B): ONE-WAY ANOVA: Comparison of teaching effectiveness based on teaching experience

Dimensions	WORK EXPERIENCE						F	P
	1-10 years		11-20 years		Above 21years			
	Mean	SD	Mean	SD	Mean	SD		
Academic & professional knowledge	20.8	2.77	21.0	2.63	20.5	2.54	.636	.530
Preparation & presentation of lesson plan	101.4	11.69	102.8	10.84	92.9	11.36	1.012	.364
Attitude towards students, teachers, colleagues, head of institution	63.1	6.55	64.1	6.40	60.1	6.60	1.394	.249
Use of motivation,	28.1	3.97	29.9	3.76	31.5	3.82	3.273	.039*

reward and punishment and interest in all round development of students								
Result, feedback accountability	7.0	1.64	7.4	1.38	7.9	1.55	3.368	.035*
Personal qualities	57.1	6.33	57.3	6.06	56.0	6.27	.759	.469
TES-Total	277.4	28.64	282	27.37	268.9	28.88	1.394	.249

*Significant level is at P<0.05

Table 4.3.B (1): Multiple Comparison of teaching effectiveness based on teaching experience: Tukey HSD

Sl. No	Areas	Groups					
		(1 – 10). (11 – 20) work experience		(1 – 10) (above 21 years) work experience		(11 – 20). (above 21 years) work experience	
		Mean difference	P	Mean difference	P	Mean difference	P
1	TES-I	.120	.904	.326	.512	.207	.723
2	TES-II	1.595	.370	1.430	.492	-.165	.989
3	TES-III	1.005	.308	1.080	.299	.076	.993
4	TES-IV	1.023*	.034*	1.043*	.036*	.288	.731
5	TES-V	.297	.148	-.073	.901	1.070*	.042*
6	TES-VI	.663	.568	.796	.485	.133	.976
	Total TES	4.434	.296	4.602	.312	.169	.998

*The mean difference is significant at the 0.05 level

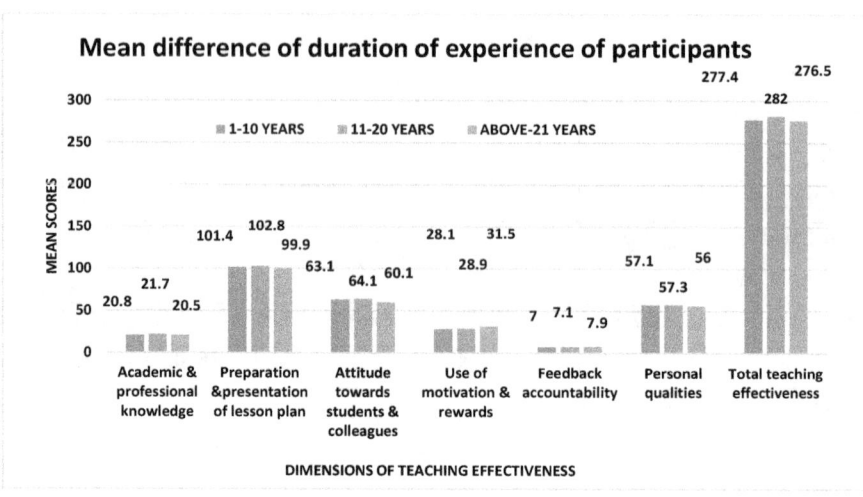

Fig.4.3 (B): Graphical representation of teaching effectiveness based on experience

Interpretation:

As determined by one way **ANOVA** test (F=1.394, p=.249) **Table 4.3 (B)**, it can be stated that there is no statistically significant difference in total teaching effectiveness based on the duration of the experience. So, the hypothesis **(Ho3)** is accepted. Also, Tuckey's post hoc test regarding total teaching effectiveness of different groups of experiences does not signify any significant difference.

From **Table 4.3 (B)** it can be noticed that the total mean score of 1-10, 11-20 are **277.4 and 282** accordingly which indicates a high level of effectiveness **(as mentioned table 3.8)**. It means that effectiveness increases with experience as they can continue to expand their expertise throughout their careers. A study conducted by **Kini & Podolsky (2016)** also supported this point. Moreover, teachers of 1-10 and 11-20 years' experience have better teaching effectiveness because they are fully acquainted with the computer knowledge, energetic and enthusiasm to organize seminars, workshops with technical connectivity. This result may be explained as follows; relatively new teachers are more enthusiastic to teach what they learned during their education and want to deliver as efficiently as possible, and teachers with more experience can automatically foster effectively due to their long years of working life. But, above 21 years of experience shows the average level of effectiveness in the **total mean score (268.9) (as mentioned in table 3.8)**. In this regard, **Dilci (2012)** reports that seniority does not lead to any difference in teaching efficacy **(cited by Bedir, 2015)**. Sometimes, more experienced teachers show a moderate level of effectiveness because they may have a lack of competence in handling computer-assisted instructions and the internet while teaching. Moreover, this may be because the teachers are more lethargic and aloofness and also stagnant in organizing co-curricular activities in the institutions due to the increase of age.

However, in two dimensions of the teaching effectiveness scale namely, the **use of motivation reward punishment** and **all-round development of students** ($F=3.273$, $p=.039$) and **feedback accountability** ($F=3.368$, $p=.035$), a statistically significant difference in mean score is found by the one way **ANOVA**. It is found that in both the dimensions; above 21 years' experience teachers have significantly higher mean scores than 1-10 and 11-20 years. Tuckey's post hoc test in table **4.3.B (1)** revealed an honestly significant difference in teaching effectiveness among the groups of (1 – 10). (11 – 20) work experience and (1 – 10). (21 – 30) work experience in the **use of motivation reward** and **punishment and all-round development of students**. It means that more experienced teachers may foster better competency of providing guidance services, motivational opportunities to students. Moreover, they may have the proper knowledge to use of teaching-learning material aids and apply need base remedial measures. Similarly, it also found that there exists a significant difference in teaching effectiveness among (11 – 20) and above 21 years of work experience in feedback accountability dimensions. Another possible explanation is that the teachers with more experience may have full knowledge of subject-matter, adequate cooperation in staff meetings and can provide feedback to students regarding performance. A study propounded by **Kalita (2012)** assessed that teaching experience is also considered as an important requirement for teaching effectiveness.

As total mean scores in table **4.3 (B)** stated that teachers with 11-20 years of teaching experience have a better level of effectiveness than 1-10 and above 21 years. The results are consistent with the previous findings. A study conducted by **Shakir (2013)** found teachers who have 11-20 years of experience are more effective than who have 1-10 years of experience. Again, **Rani & Devi (2015)** suggested in the study that teachers possessing above 10 years of teaching experience are more effective in teaching as a comparison to teachers below 10 years' experience of Senior Secondary School Teachers. Likewise, **Dash & Barman (2016)** found the study that mean scores of teaching experience groups has an impact on the effectiveness of teaching. A major finding of the study conducted by **Arya & Singh (2016)** signified that no significant difference exists in teacher effectiveness concerning teaching experiences. Identically, **Kaur & Sharma (2015)** initiated that teacher effectiveness did not get affected by teaching experiences.

Objective No.4: To compare the perception of organizational climate of male and female college teachers.

(Ho4) There will be no significant difference in the perception of organizational climate of male and female college teachers.

Table 4.4 (A): Level of organizational climate on the basis of gender

OCQ-Groups	Gender					
	Male		Female		Total	
	Count	%	Count	%	Count	%
Very low	3	1.1	10	3.7	13	2.4
Low	69	25.4	90	33.1	159	29.2
Average	53	19.1	112	41.2	246	45.2
High	134	49.3	50	18.0	103	18.6
Very high	15	5.1	12	4.0	27	4.6
Total	274	100.0	274	100.0	548	100.0

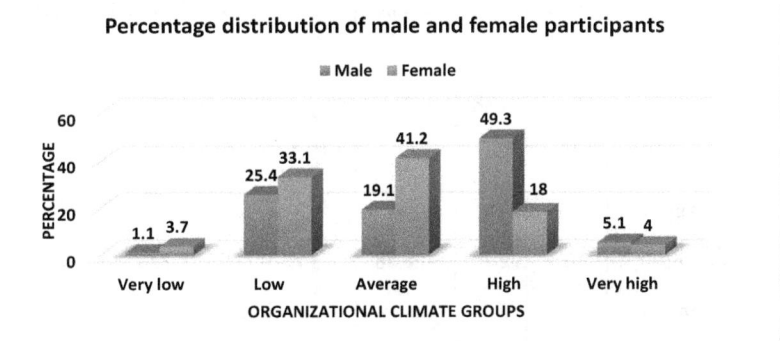

Fig.4.4 (A): Percentage distribution of perception of organizational climate on the basis of gender

Table 4.4 (A) shows that 1.1% of male college teachers have a very low perception towards organizational climate, 25.4% have low, 19.1% have average, 49.3% have high, and 5.1% have a very high level of organizational climate. Again, 3.7% of female college teachers have a very low-level organizational climate, 33.1% have low, 41.2% have average, 18.0% have high and 4.0% have a very high level of perception of organizational climate. This means that male college teachers mostly experience a better perception of organizational climate as compared to female teachers.

Table 4.4 (B): Comparison of the perception of organizational climate on the basis of gender

Sl. No	Areas	Male			Female			z	P
		Mean	SD	Mean Rank	Mean	SD	Mean Rank		
1	Physical Environment	18.0	3.10	292.31	17.1	3.43	252.69	-2.953	.003**
2	Library Facilities	9.1	2.65	277.64	8.7	2.40	267.36	-.265	.724
3	Reward System	12.8	2.34	274.80	12.8	2.48	270.20	-.344	.731
4	Relationship with Colleagues	13.6	3.50	293.22	10.6	3.16	251.78	-3.090	.002**
5	Support System	16.4	2.76	266.86	15.7	3.06	278.14	-.841	.400
6	Academic Climate	25.2	3.51	273.41	23.1	3.20	271.59	-.135	.892
	Total	95.2	9.41	290.89	88.0	10.04	254.11	-2.731	.006**

** Correlation is significant at the 0.01 level (2-tailed).

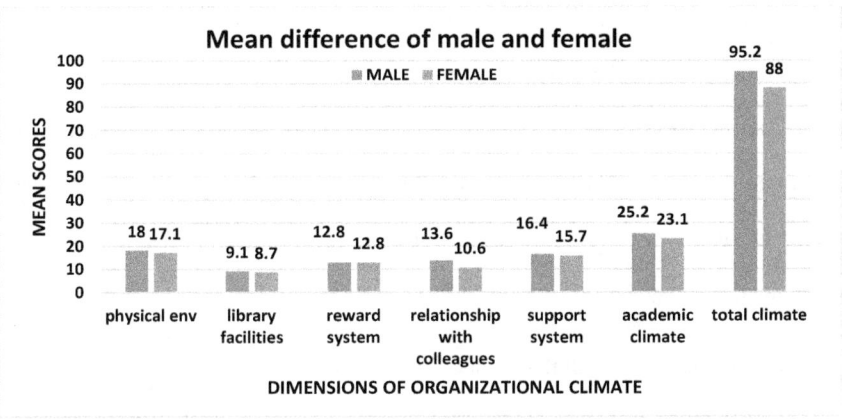

Fig.4.4 (B): Graphical representation of the perception of organizational climate based on gender

Interpretation:

From **Table4.4 (B)** 'Z' value we can say that the result is significant and it indicates there is a statistically significant difference in terms of the total means core of the perception of organizational climate for the male and female college teachers. So, the hypothesis **(Ho4)** is rejected. The total mean score of male and female college teachers' is **95.2 and 88.0** accordingly which signifies the positively favourable and moderate level of organizational climate **(as mentioned in table 3.12)**. Moreover, 'Z' value found to be statistically significant at $P<0.01$ in two dimensions of organizational climate (namely psychological environment, and relationship with colleagues).

In, physical environment dimensions the male participants have a statistically significant higher mean score **(18.0)** than the female participants **(17.1)**. This is because there is a higher possibility among female teachers to influence environmental aspects. The reason behind the female teachers may be they are affected by poor infrastructure facilities, lack of cleanliness and hygiene, unhealthy circumstances regarding a high level of noise which may lead to frustration, nervousness. Uniformly, (in relationship with colleagues 'dimensions) the male participants yield a statistically significant higher mean score (11.6) than female counterparts (10.6). These aspects indicating that they have a proper sense of direction of providing helping hands to each other may hold beliefs to fulfil their responsibilities with co-workers and may have a lack of professional jealousy.

The result indicated that both the genders have a significant influence on organisational climate. This seems consistent with prior research of **Khasawneh (2013)** that reported statistically significant differences in the perception of organizational climate by gender.

Objective No.5: To compare the perception of organizational climate of rural and urban college teachers.

(Ho5) There will be no significant difference in the perception of organizational climate of rural and urban college teachers.

Table 4.5 (A): Level of the perception of the perception of organizational climate on the basis of locality

OCQ-Groups	Locality					
	Rural		Urban		Total	
	Count	%	Count	%	Count	%
Very low	9	3.3	4	1.5	13	2.4
Low	97	35.7	62	22.8	159	29.2
Average	113	41.2	134	49.3	247	45.2
High	49	18.0	53	19.1	102	18.6
Very high	6	1.8	21	7.4	27	4.6
Total	274	100.0	274	100.0	548	100.0

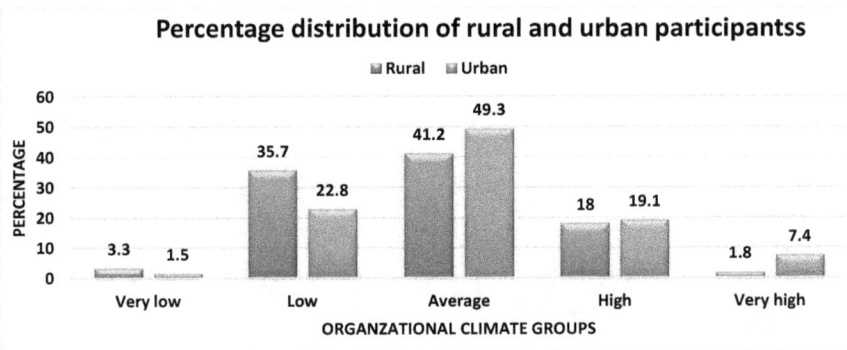

Fig.4.5 (A): Percentage distribution of the perception of organizational climate on the basis of locality

Table4.5 (A) identifies that 3.3% of rural college teachers have perceived a very low level of organizational climate, 35.7% have a low level, 41.2% average, and 18.0% have a high and 1.8% very high level of organizational climate. Additionally, 1.5% urban college teachers reflect a very low level, 22.8% shows low level, 49.3% have average level, and 19.1% have high level and 7.4% experience very high level of organizational climate. This proves that college teachers comprising both localities have a moderate favourable perception of organizational climate.

Table 4.5 (B): Comparison of the perception of organizational climate on the basis of locality

Sl. No	Areas	Rural			Urban			"z"	P
		Mean	SD	Mean Rank	Mean	SD	Mean Rank		
1	Physical Environment	16.5	3.18	220.26	18.6	3.09	324.74	-7.787	.000**
2	Library Facilities	9.0	2.66	274.49	8.9	2.36	270.51	-.298	.766
3	Reward System	12.8	2.49	275.56	12.7	2.33	269.44	-.457	.648

4	Relationship with Colleagues	10.8	3.47	259.50	11.3	3.25	285.50	-1.939	.043*
5	Support System	15.8	2.82	288.52	15.3	2.99	256.48	-2.390	.037*
6	Academic Climate	22.8	3.52	252.40	23.6	3.14	292.60	-2.998	.003**
	Total	87.8	9.44	252.76	90.4	9.95	292.24	-2.931	.003**

*Significant level is at P<0.05
**Significant level is at P<0.01

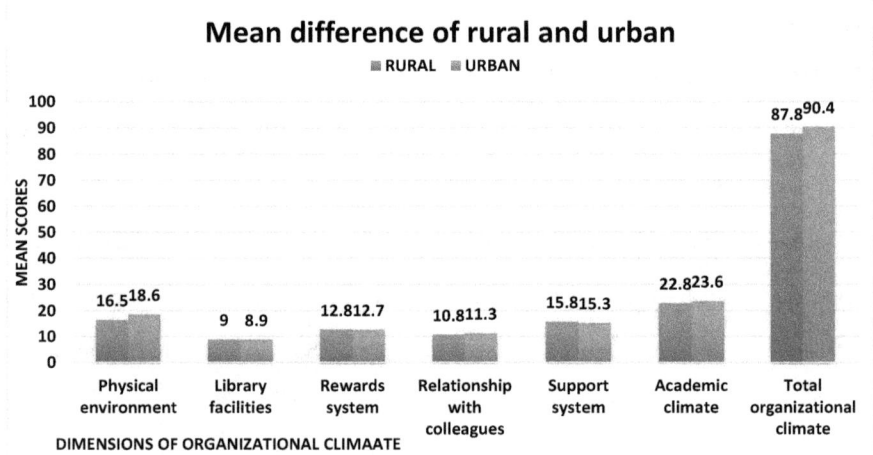

Fig.4.5 (B): Graphical representation of the perception of organizational climate based on locality

Interpretation:

From the 'Z' value of the above **Table 4.5 (B),** it can be observed that statistically significant differences exist between the total mean score of the perception of organizational climate based on rural and urban areas. So, the hypothesis **(Ho5)** is rejected. Besides, it can be assumed that 'Z' value significant at P<0.01 and P<0.05 in four dimensions of organizational climate questionnaire (namely physical environment, relationship with colleagues, support system and academic climate).

The total mean score of rural and urban teachers lies in **87.8 and 90.4** accordingly which estimates a **moderately favourable climate (as mentioned in Table 3.12)**. It can be noticed that urban-based college teachers have higher mean scores regarding the three dimensions of organizational climate specifically, **physical environment (18.6), relationship with colleagues (11.3)** and **academic climate (23.6)** compared to rural teachers [**physical environment (16.5), relationship with colleagues (10.8) and academic climate (22.8)**]. This is because the organizational climate of urban areas may have sufficient infrastructural facilities with proper arrangement of furniture in the classrooms and plenty of teaching materials. Another point found in the study conducted by **Chaithra & Hiremath (2018)** that the major problems faced by rural school teachers are drinking water, lack of teaching aids, no sufficient building for the school, lack of coordination, and lack of freedom for free discussion. Moreover, the teacher's perception to develop positive relationships with colleagues is very crucial. The teachers in urban college can actively co-operate with colleagues for organizing co-curricular activities. The result indicated that there is a slightly higher mean score in the three dimensions of organisational climate regarding urban college teachers and also locality did significant impact on climate settings. But, (support system dimensions), rural teachers signify a slightly higher mean score in comparison to urban teachers. This means that rural teachers can grasp better provision to participate in refresher courses, financial aids may provide to organize educational seminars, workshops in college. It can also be noticed that (in the dimensions of library facilities, reward system) both the locality indicates almost the same level of mean score.

The study is found to be consistent with **Ghose & Guha (2016)** who examined the significant difference between rural and urban teachers perception of organisational climate. Consequently, **Kumar & Kaur (2017)** found a significant difference among locality concerning the perception of organizational climate of engineering college teachers.

Objective No.6: To compare the perception of organizational climate of college teachers based on length of experience.

(Ho6) There will be no significant difference in the perception of organizational climate of college teachers based on the duration of experience.

Table 4.6 (A): Level of the perception of organizational climate based on teaching experience

OCQ-Groups	Teaching experience							
	1-10 Years		11-20 Years		Above 21 Years		Total	
	Count	%	Count	%	Count	%	Count	%
Very low	6	4.0	4	1.8	3	1.8	13	2.4
Low	30	19.9	67	30.0	62	36.5	159	29.2
Average	81	53.6	98	43.9	67	39.4	246	45.2
High	22	13.9	48	21.5	32	18.8	102	18.6
Very high	14	8.6	6	2.7	8	3.5	28	4.6
Total	153	100.0	223	100.0	172	100.0	548	100.0

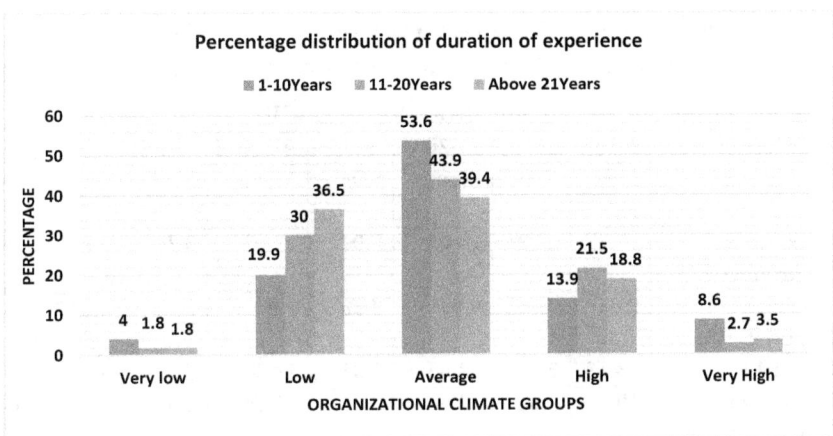

Fig.4.6 (A): Percentage distribution of the perception of organizational climate based on experience

Table4.6 (A) indicates that 4% of teachers with 1-10 years of teaching experience have a very low level of the perception of organizational climate, 19.9% low level, 53.6% have average level, 13.9% have a high level and 8.6% have a very high level of perception of organizational climate. Again, 1.8% of teachers with 11-20 years have a very low level of organizational climate, 30% have a low level, 43.9% have average, 21.5% have high and 2.7% have a very high level of organizational climate. Hence, 1.8% of teachers with above 21 years have a very low level of organizational climate, 36.5% have low, 39.4% have average, 18.8% have high and 3.5% have a very high level of organizational climate. This means that teachers with 1-10, 11-20 and above 21 years teaching experience have proved a moderate favourable organizational climate.

Table 4.6 (B): ONE-WAY ANOVA: Comparison of the perception of organizational climate based on duration of experience.

AREAS	WORK EXPERIENCE						F	P
	1-10 years		11-20 years		Above 21 years			
	Mean	SD	Mean	SD	Mean	SD		
Physical Environment	17.37	3.22	18.05	2.94	17.05	3.70	4.871	.008*
Library Facilities	8.68	2.61	9.04	2.26	9.09	2.72	1.279	.279
Reward System	13.13	2.53	12.90	2.34	12.36	2.33	4.479	.012*
Relationship with colleagues	10.74	3.64	10.88	3.15	11.75	3.31	4.392	.013*
Support System	15.71	2.92	15.26	3.26	15.76	2.86	1.732	.178
Academic Climate	23.46	3.28	22.94	3.09	23.24	3.73	1.150	.318
OCQ-Total	90.10	18.20	88.97	17.04	88.34	18.65	1.321	.268

*Significant level is at P<0.05

Table 4.6.B (1): Multiple Comparisons of the perception of organizational climate based on duration of experience: Tukey HSD

AREAS	Work experience groups					
	(1-10). (11-20) work experience		(1-10). (above-21) work experience		(11-20). (above-21) work experience	
	Mean Difference	P	Mean Difference	P	Mean Difference	P
Physical Environment	-.683	.118	.324	.650	1.007*	.007*
Library Facilities	-.358	.367	-.412	.308	-.054	.976
Reward System	.224	.647	1.767*	.002*	.543	.068
Relationship with colleagues	.977*	.016*	1.207*	.041*	-.070	.977
Support System	.444	.317	-.050	.987	-.494	.219
Academic Climate	.526	.298	.222	.824	-.304	.647
Total	1.131	1.030	1.758	.243	.627	.803

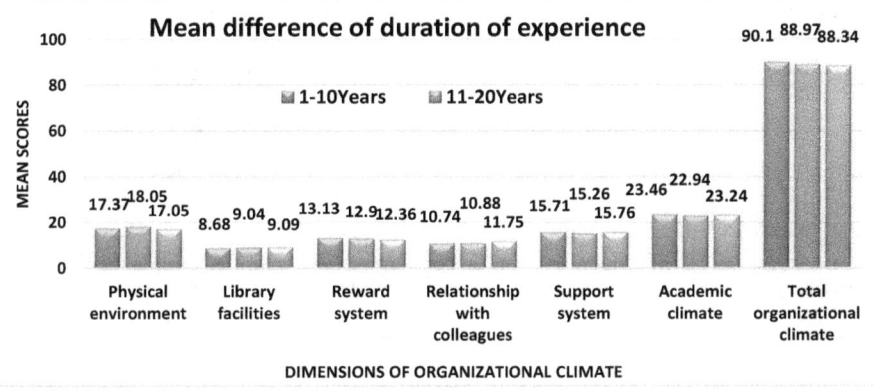

Fig.4.6 (B): Graphical representation of the perception of organizational climate based on experience

Interpretation:

As determined by one way **ANOVA** test (F=1.321, p=.268) in **Table 4.6 (B)**, it can be stated that there is a statistically no significant difference in the perception of organizational climate based on the duration of the experience. So, the hypothesis **(Ho6)** is accepted. Still, it can be noticed that the total mean score of 11-20 years shows marginally higher in the **physical environment dimensions (F=4.871, p=.008)** of organizational climate. This is because the teachers with 11-20 years of experience may more compatible with the existing climate of the organization and they can adjust with the inconvenient circumstances. Also, in the **reward system dimensions**, 1 – 10 years' experience teachers found a high mean score **(F=4.479, p=.012)** as compared to their counterparts. This is obvious that while entering the job the employee may keep themselves energetic and can enthusiastically manage the works. Their good work may recognize efficiently by all senior members of the organization. Likewise, in the aspects of other dimensions i.e. **Relationship with Colleagues**, of above 21 years treasure high mean score **(F=4.392, p=.013)** than the other two groups of experience. With increasing age/experience, their maturity level gets promoted and they can help each other to fulfil their professional expectations without any obstruction. Tuckey's post hoc test in table **4.6.B (1)** identified the honestly significant difference of the perception of organizational climate among the groups of (1 – 10), (11 – 20) and (1 – 10), above 21 years work experience regarding relationship with colleagues dimensions; difference in (1 – 10), (above 21 years) work experience in the dimensions of rewards systems; and simultaneously, in physical environment there exist difference between (11 – 20) and (above 21 years) of work experience. Hence, the total result from Tuckey's post hoc test signifies no significant difference regarding the total perception of organizational climate of different groups of experiences. Also, the total mean score of 1-10 Years indicates (90.10), 11-20 years (88.97) and above 21 years (88.34) of experience teachers foster a moderate favourable perception of organizational climate at each level **(as mentioned in table 3.12)**.

The above results are consistent with **Panneerselvam & Muthamizhselvan (2015)** who found that teaching experience does not influence on the perception of organizational climate. Also, the study propounded by **Manikandan (2014)** exhibits that the length of experience of the teachers does not exist a noticeable impact on the perception of organizational climate.

Objective No.7: To compare the mental health of male and female college teachers.

(Ho7) There will be no significant difference in the mental health of male and female college teachers.

Table 4.7 (A): Level of mental health based on gender

EMHI-Groups	Gender					
	Male		Female		Total	
	Count	%	Count	%	Count	%
Very low	55	20.3	66	23.9	139	25.6
Low	19	6.6	47	17.3	132	24.3
Average	75	27.5	72	26.5	137	25.2
High	102	37.5	57	21.0	85	15.3
Very high	23	8.1	32	11.4	55	9.7
Total	274	100.0	274	100.0	548	100.0

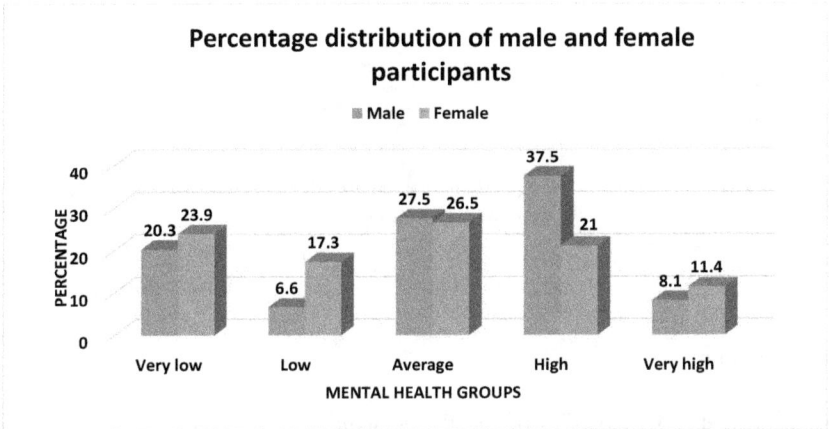

Fig.4.7 (A): Percentage distribution of mental health based on gender

Table 4.7 (A) shows that 20.3% of male college teachers have a very low level of mental health, 6.6% have a low level, 27.5% have an average level, 37.5% have a high level and 8.15% have signified a very high level of mental health. 23.9% of female college teachers have a very low level of mental health, 17.3% have a low level, 26.5% have an average level, 21% have a high level and 11.4% have a very high level of mental health status. This means that corresponding to male college teachers' maximum percentage lies at a high level so it can be said that male college teachers have satisfactory mental health status. Whereas, female college teachers exhibit moderate mental health conditions.

Table 4.7 (B): Comparison of mental health based on gender

Tools	Male			Female			"Z"	Significant (2-tailed)
	Mean	SD	Mean Ranks	Mean	SD	Mean Ranks		
EMHI	22.6	3.68	290.35	17.6	4.30	254.65	-2.658	.008*

*Significant level is at P<0.05

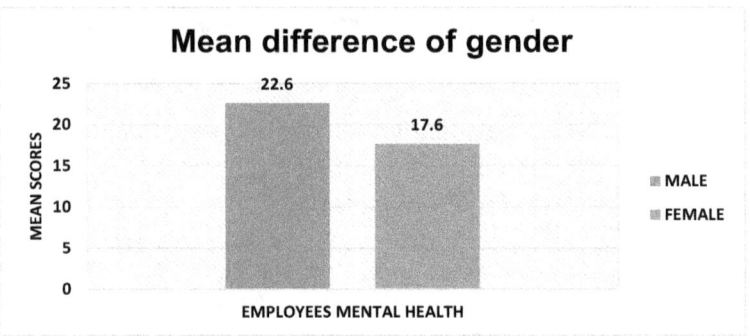

Fig.4.7 (B): Graphical representation mental health based on gender

Interpretation:

The above **Table 4.7 (B)** 'Z' score inculcated significant difference between male and female college teachers in mental health status. The total mean score of male college teachers **(22.6)** signify **higher** mental health status than female counterparts **(17.6)** which indicates a **medium** level of mental health **(as mentioned in Table 3.15)**. That means male teachers possess good mental health in comparison to female teachers. The probable reason is that male teacher is more capable of coping with stress in comparison to females. Moreover, a working female may frequently have to maintain proper work-life balance which has a great impact on their physiological health. The result encompasses that gender has a significant influence on mental health. So, the hypothesis (Ho7) is rejected.

The results are in line with the study conducted by **Gorsy, Panwar& Kumar (2015)** who showed significant gender differences in the mental health of government school teachers. Again, **Prathima & Kulsum (2013), Mishra (2018)** and **Pathak (2015)** examined significant gender distinction regarding the mental health of secondary/ primary school teachers. A study carried out by **Manikandan (2012)** and **Dagar & Mathur (2016)** explored male teachers hold a supreme level of mental health condition in school settings.

Objective No.8: To compare the mental health of rural and urban college teachers.

Ho8) There will be no significant difference in the mental health of rural and urban college teachers.

Table 4.8 (A): **Level of mental health based on locality**

EMHI-Groups	Gender					
	Urban		Rural		Total	
	Count	%	Count	%	Count	%
Very low	41	15.1	57	21.0	139	25.6
Low	49	18.0	83	30.5	132	24.3
Average	64	23.2	98	36.0	137	25.2
High	80	29.4	21	7.4	85	15.3
Very high	40	14.3	15	5.1	55	9.7
Total	274	100.0	274	100.0	548	100.0

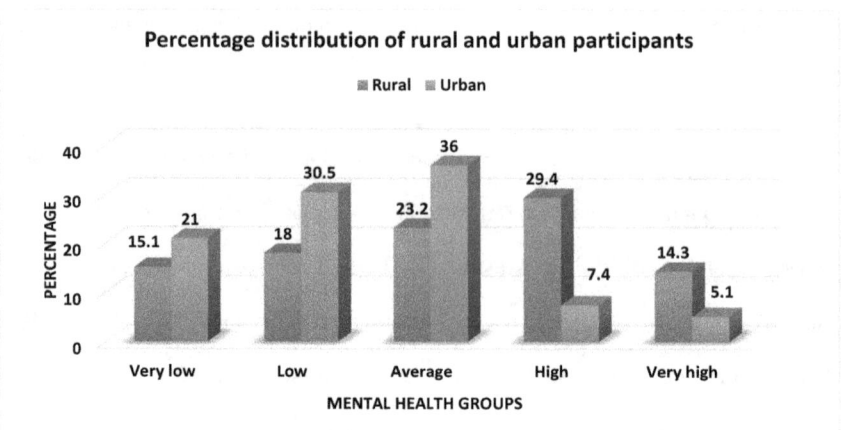

Fig.4.8 (A): Percentage distribution of mental health based on locality

Table4.8 (A) shows that 15.1% of urban college teachers have a very low level of mental health, 18% have a low level, 23.2% have an average level, 29.4% have a high level and 14.3% have a very high level of mental health. Rural college teachers with 21% have a very low level of mental health, 30.5% have a low level, 36% have average level, 7.4% have high and 5.1% have a very high level of mental health. This signifies that urban college teachers shows a higher percentage of favourable mental health. But, the rural college teachers have experience with moderate favourable mental health.

Table 4.8 (B): Comparison of mental health status based on Locality

Tools	Rural			Urban			"Z"	Significant (2-tailed)
	Mean	SD	Mean Ranks	Mean	SD	Mean Ranks		
EMHI	16.7	4.04	217.51	22.0	3.50	327.49	-8.186	.000**

**Significant level is at P<0.01

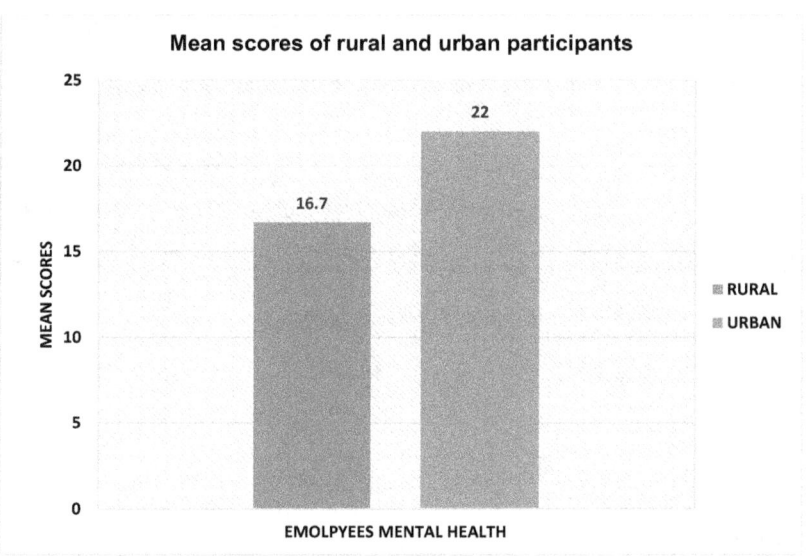

Fig.4.8 (B): Graphical representation mental health status based on Locality

Interpretation:

Table 4.8 (B) shows highly significant differences in mental health between rural and urban teachers. The mean value of rural teachers with regards to mental health is (16.7) which lies **a medium level** of health status and the mean value of **urban** teachers is (22.0) and it covers the **high level** of mental health (**as mentioned in Table 3.15**). It suggested that urban college teachers did better in mental health status compared to rural teachers. The Z value found to be –8.186. The S.D. values of rural and urban teachers are found to be 4.04 and 3.50 respectively. The result indicated that locality plays a significant influence on mental health. So, the hypothesis (**Ho8**) is rejected. The possible reason for better mental health condition in urban areas is that the teachers may have a better adequate perseverance regarding working conditions. They may have positive vibes concerning professional recognition. In contrast to a rural school, the working conditions sometimes may not be adequate due to unhealthy disciplinary policies, too much workload due to a lack of sufficient teaching staff. These are the aspects that may contribute to differences between rural and urban college teachers' mental health status.

The above result supported by **Gorsy, Panwar & Kumar (2015)** who reported that teachers regarding urban areas revealed a good quality of mental health in comparison to rural area. Similarly, **Pandhi and Rajendra (2010)** also displayed that the mental health of secondary school teachers in rural areas significantly differs from the urban areas.

Objective No.9: To compare the mental health of college teachers with respect to the duration of experience.

(Ho9): There will be no significant difference in the mental health of college teachers on the basis of duration of the experience.

Table 4.9 (A): Level of mental health based on teaching experience

EMHI-Groups	Teaching experience							
	1-10 Years		11-20 Years		Above 21 Years		Total	
	Count	%	Count	%	Count	%	Count	%
Very low	20	12.6	49	22.0	38	22.4	139	25.6
Low	33	21.9	55	24.7	44	25.9	132	24.3
Average	38	25.2	59	26.5	40	23.5	137	25.2
High	52	34.4	32	14.3	33	18.8	85	15.3
Very high	10	6.0	28	12.6	17	9.4	55	9.7
Total	153	100.0	223	100.0	172	100.0	548	100.0

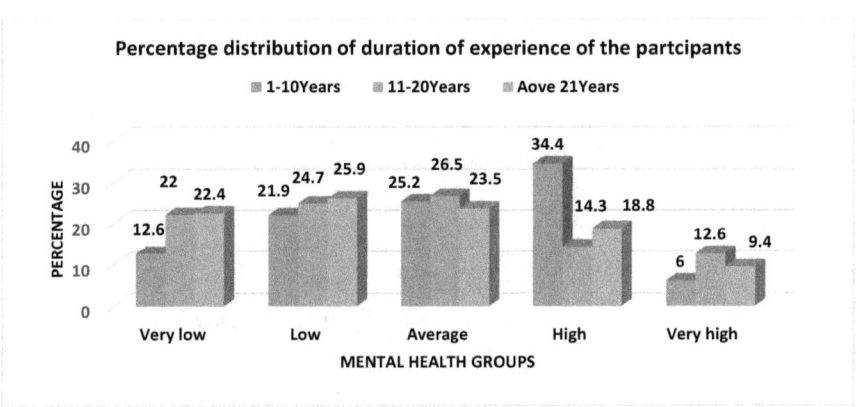

Fig.4.9 (A): Percentage distribution of mental health based on teaching experience

Table 4.9 (A) shows that 12.6% of college teachers with 1-10 years of teaching experience have a very low level of mental health, 21.9% low level, 25.2% have average level, 34.4% have a high level and 6% have a very high level of mental health. College teachers with 11-20 years have 22% very low level of mental health, 24.7% low level, 26.5% have average level, 14.3% have a high level and 12.6% have a very high level of mental health. Again, 22.4% of college teachers above 21 years have a very low level of mental health, 25.9% low level, 23.5% have average level, 18.8% have high level, and 9.4% have a very high level of mental health. This means that college teachers with 1-10 years of teaching experience are confronting with higher favourable mental health. Hence, college teachers with 11-20 years have moderate favourable mental health and above 21 years shown slightly unfavourable mental health.

Table 4.9 (B): ONE-WAY ANOVA: Comparison of mental health based on duration of experience

	Work Experience						F	P-value
EMHI	1-10		11-20		Above-21			
	Mean	SD	Mean	SD	Mean	SD		
	22.5	4.057	19.70	4.061	17.79	3.866	4.824	.008*

*mean difference is significant at the 0.05 level.

Table 4.9.B (1): Multiple Comparisons of mental health based on duration of experience: Tukey HSD

TOOLS	Groups					
	(1-10).(11-20) work experience		(1-10).(above-21)work experience		(11-20).(above-21)work experience	
EMHI	Mean Difference	P	Mean Difference	P	Mean Difference	P
	1.272*	.008*	1.032*	.046*	-.240	.826

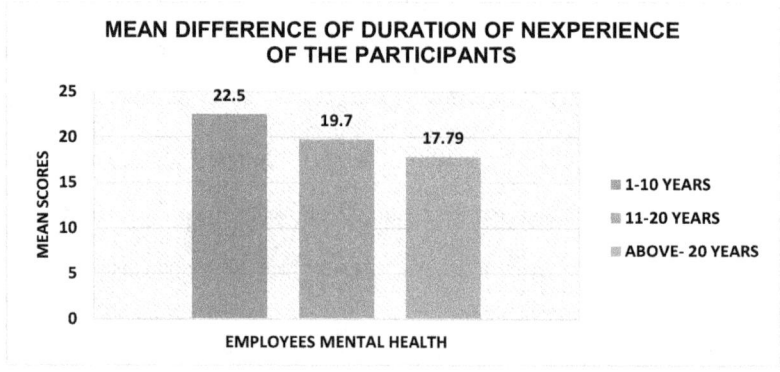

Fig.4.9 (B): Graphical representation of mental health based on experience

Interpretation:

As observed by one way **ANOVA** test (F=4.824, p=008.) in **Table 4.9(B)**, it can be noticed that there is a statistically significant difference in the mental health status of college teachers based on the duration of the experience. The total mean score of 1-10 years' experience **(22.5)** teachers indicates the **slightly high level** in comparison to 11-20 **(19.7)** and above 21 **years** of **experience (17.79)** which lies a **medium level** of mental health **(as mentioned in Table 3.15)**. This supports that teaching experience has a significant impact on the mental health of college teachers. Tuckey's post hoc test in table **4.9.B**.1 identified the honestly significant difference of mental health among the groups of (1 – 10), (11 – 20) and (1-10) and above 20 years of work experience. This is because if the experience increases by years the teachers' mental health may slightly deteriorate. The probable reason is that they may have to maintain proper family work-life balance, excess workload regarding the responsibility of the workplace. Moreover, due to the increase of age, some psycho-physiological health-related problems may occur which greatly impact the mental health condition. So, the result indicated that the duration of experience has a significant impact on the mental health of college teachers. So, the hypothesis, **(Ho9)** is rejected.

The result is compatible with the study conducted by **Rathee (2017)** who found more experienced teachers exhibit poor mental health in comparison to fewer experienced teachers. Similarly, **Khatun (2013)** revealed a significant difference in teaching experience regarding the mental health of secondary level teachers. **Pradhan (2016)** found a partial significant difference in the mental health of Tribal and Non-Tribal teachers with teaching experience variation.

Objective No.10: To compare the attitude towards ICT of male and female college teachers.

(Ho10) There will be no difference in the attitude towards ICT of male and female college teachers.

Table 4.10 (A): Level of attitude towards ICT based on gender

ATICT-Groups	Gender					
	Male		Female		Total	
	Count	%	Count	%	Count	%
Very low	4	1.5	2	.7	6	1.1
Low	75	27.6	65	23.9	140	25.7
Average	137	50.4	161	59.2	298	54.8
High	50	18.4	32	11.8	82	15.1
Very high	8	2.2	14	4.4	22	3.3
Total	274	100.0	274	100.0	548	100.0

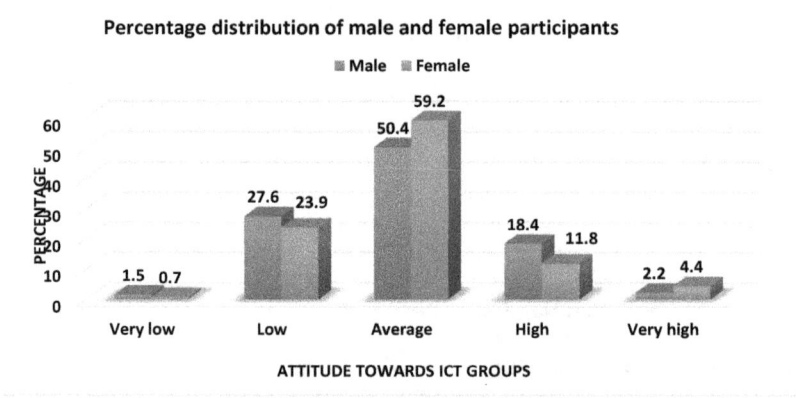

Fig.4.10 (A): Percentage distribution of attitude towards ICT based on gender

Table 4.10(A) shows that 1.5% of male college teachers have a very low level of attitude towards ICT, 27.6% have a low level, 50.4% have an average level, 18.4% have a high level and 2.2% have a very high level of attitude towards ICT. Female college teachers with 0.7% have a very low level of attitude towards ICT, 23.9% have low levels, 59.2% have average level, 11.8% have high and 4.4% have very high levels of attitude towards ICT. This signifies that both genders have faced moderately favourable attitude towards ICT.

Table 4.10 (B): Comparison of attitude towards ICT based on gender

Sl. No	Areas	Male			Female			"z"	P
		Mean	SD	Mean Rank	Mean	SD	Mean Rank		
1	Productivity of teaching	23.8	3.82	257.30	25.2	4.12	287.70	2.265	.024*
2	Usefulness for students	24.6	3.06	276.69	24.4	3.62	268.31	.628	.530
3	Teachers interest and acceptance	29.9	3.61	275.17	29.5	4.35	269.83	.398	.691
	Total	78.3	7.92	264.71	78.1	9.63	280.29	1.157	.247

*mean difference is significant at the 0.05 level.

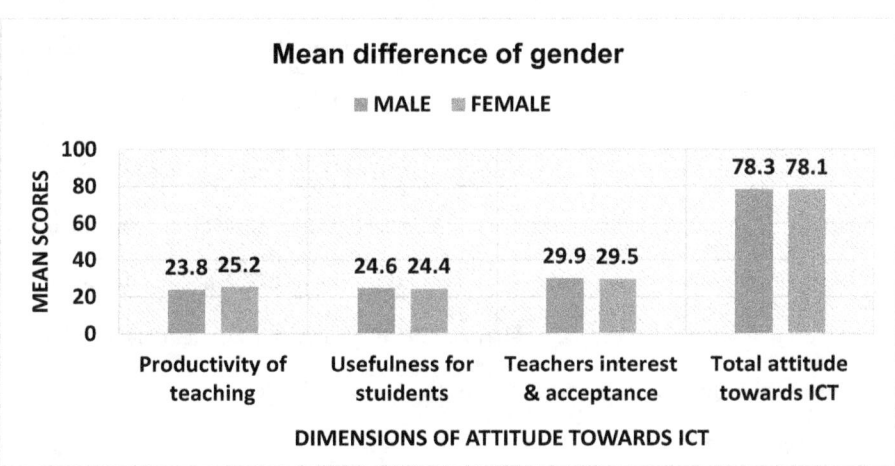

Fig.4.10 (B): Graphical representation of attitude towards ICT based on gender

Interpretation:

From the above **Table 4.10(B)** total 'Z' score it indicated no significant difference between male and female college teachers concerning attitude towards ICT. So, the hypothesis **(Ho10)** is accepted. The total mean score of male and female participants is **(78.3)** and **(78.1)** respectively which signifies a **moderately favourable attitude** towards ICT. This means both the gender indicates the same level of attitude towards ICT **(mentioned in table 3.19)**. The findings revealed that both genders have a positive attitude towards the use of ICT in instructional teaching to enhance academic performance. The majority of the respondents revealed that they frequently use ICT for the purpose like keeping track of student's performance, accessing information and educational materials, preparing a lesson plan, doing presentations relevant to topics to make lessons more motivating for the learner. The respondents also felt that the teacher's prior knowledge and skill in ICT is important for the benefit of the students.

But, in the dimensions of **(productivity of teaching)**, female teacher's mean scores area little bit more as compare to male. The difference also seems as significant. This is due to the reason that the majority of female respondents have better ICT integrated application package into their classrooms. They may also more comfortable using relevant resources for the teaching-learning process in the classroom through ICT.

The above results supported by **Olafare et al. (2017)** who found no significant gender influence in lecturers' attitudes toward the use of ICT in Nigeria. **Nagamani & Muthuswamy (2013)** also evaluated that the utilization of ICT is not affected by gender in secondary school teachers. **Mahajan (2016)** also found no significant difference between the attitudes of teachers towards the use of technology in teaching concerning their gender.

Objective No.11: To compare the attitude towards ICT of rural and urban college teachers.

(Ho11) There will be no difference in the attitude towards ICT of rural and urban college teachers.

Table 4.11 (A): Level of attitude towards ICT based on locality

ATICT-Groups	Locality					
	Rural		Urban		Total	
	Count	%	Count	%	Count	%
Very low	3	1.1	3	1.1	6	1.1
Low	71	26.1	69	25.4	140	25.7
Average	155	57.0	143	52.6	298	54.8
High	37	13.2	47	16.9	84	15.1
Very high	8	2.6	12	4.0	20	3.3
Total	274	100.0	274	100.0	548	100.0

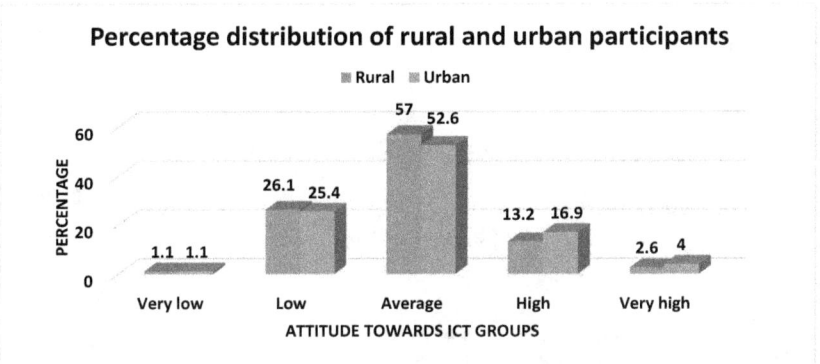

Fig.4.11 (A): Percentage distribution of attitude towards ICT based on locality

Table 4.11(A) shows that 1.1% of rural college teachers have a very low level of attitude towards ICT, 26.1% have low levels, 57% have average levels, 13.1% have high levels and 2.6% have very high level of attitude towards ICT. Urban college teachers with 1.1% have a very low level of attitude towards ICT, 25.4% have low level, 52.6% have average level, 16.9% have high and 4% have very high level of attitude towards ICT. This signifies that both the locality have confronted with the moderately favourable attitude towards ICT.

Table 4.11 (B): Comparison of attitude towards ICT based on locality

Sl. No	Dimensions	Rural			Urban			"z"	P
		Mean	SD	Mean Rank	Mean	SD	Mean Rank		
1	Productivity of teaching	23.5	3.67	290.89	25.5	4.21	254.11	2.739	.006*
2	Usefulness for students	24.4	3.20	267.76	24.6	3.48	277.24	.710	.478
3	Teachers interest and acceptance	29.7	4.04	269.63	29.7	3.96	275.37	.428	.669
	Total	77.8	8.48	276.85	78.6	9.13	268.15	.646	.518

*mean difference is significant at the 0.05 level.

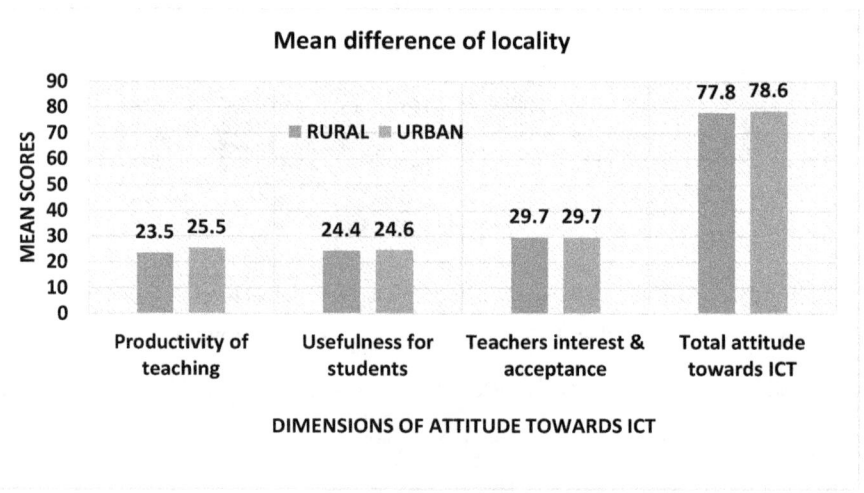

Fig.4.11 (B): Graphical representation attitude towards ICT based on locality

Interpretation:

Table 4.11(B) also confirming that overall rural and urban teachers have almost the same opinion towards ICT awareness. So, the hypothesis **(Ho11)** is accepted. The mean score of overall urban-rural teachers' falls within moderate favourable attitude level i.e. **(78.6) and (77.8) [mentioned in Table 3.19].** It shows that the urban teachers' mean scores is a little bit more as compared to the rural college teachers, but not seems as significant except dimensions **(productivity of teaching)**. In spite of non-significant differences, urban college teachers possess a higher attitude towards the application of ICT because of the availability of IT resources in teaching processes. The urban college teachers also reported that they have better training facilities respecting information technology implication in educational settings, they may more comfortable in using ICT in the classroom due to necessary instructional aides for teachers. But in the dimensions of **(usefulness for students)**, and **(teachers' interest and acceptance)**, both the areas shows almost the same level of utilization of attitude towards ICT. They also supported that knowledge of information technology can motivate teachers to improve professional advancements and also can provide relevant technological information for students. Furthermore, irregular and interrupted power supply **(Kumar & Kumar, 2018),** slow bandwidth, slower internet speeds, lack of ready access to technology may also happen to be major deterrents in the adoption of technology in developing areas **(Islahi, 2019).**

The result in line with the study of **Sridharan & Krishnakumar (2015)** who postulates no significant difference in the Attitude of teacher educators towards ICT regarding their locality of college teacher educators. **Li (2012); Zaman et al., (2018); Zhao, Xu,**

& Chen, (2017) also found that both rural and urban school teachers exhibiting a significantly positive attitude towards ICT.

Objective No. 12) To compare the attitude towards ICT of college teachers based on the duration of experience.

(Ho12) There will be no difference in attitude towards ICT of college teachers based on the duration of experience.

Table 4.12 (A): Level of attitude towards ICT based on teaching experience

ATICT-Groups	Teaching experience							
	1-10 Years		11-20 Years		Above 21 Years		Total	
	Count	%	Count	%	Count	%	Count	%
Very low	2	1.3	3	1.3	1	.6	6	1.1
Low	36	23.8	63	28.3	50	29.4	140	25.7
Average	89	58.9	117	52.5	83	48.8	298	54.8
High	23	14.6	34	15.2	27	15.3	84	15.1
Very high	3	1.3	6	2.7	11	5.9	20	3.3
Total	153	100.0	223	100.0	172	100.0	548	100.0

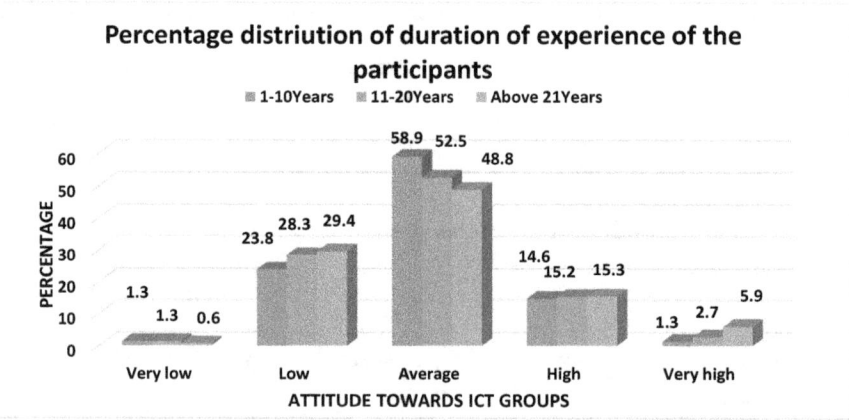

Fig.4.12 (A): Percentage distribution of attitude towards ICT based on experience

Table 4.12(A) shows that 1.3% college teachers with 1-10 years of teaching experience have a very low level of attitude towards ICT, 23.8% have low level, 58.9% have average level, 14.6% have high level and 1.3% has very high level of attitude towards ICT. College teachers with 11-20 years have a 1.3% very low level of attitude towards ICT, 28.3% low level, 52.5% have average level, 15.2% have high level, and 2.7% have a very high level of attitude towards ICT. Again, .6% of college teachers above 21 years have a very low level of, 29.4% low level, 48.8% have average level, 15.3% have high level, and 5.9% have a very high level of attitude towards ICT. This means that college teachers with 1-10, 11-20 and above 21 years of teaching experience are confronting with moderately favourable attitude towards ICT.

Table 4.12 (B): ONE-WAY ANOVA: Comparison of attitude towards ICT based on duration of experience.

AREAS	WORK EXPERIENCE						F	P
	1-10 years		11-20 years		Above 21 years			
	Mean	SD	Mean	SD	Mean	SD		
Productivity of teaching	24.40	3.033	23.85	4.271	22.85	4.301	1.034	.356
Usefulness for students	24.91	2.828	24.97	3.043	23.93	4.022	4.747	.009*
Teachers interest & acceptance	29.79	3.138	29.86	3.586	28.46	5.047	.863	.423
Total ATICT	78.70	6.243	78.68	8.191	77.12	11.174	1.847	.159

*mean difference is significant at the 0.05 level.

Table 4.12.B (1): Multiple comparison of attitude towards ICT based on duration of experience: Tukey HSD

AREAS	Groups					
	(1-10). (11-20) work experience		(1-10). (above-21) work experience		(11-20). (above-21) work experience	
	Mean Difference	P	Mean Difference	P	Mean Difference	P
Productivity of teaching	.545	.395	.550	.432	.005	1.000
Usefulness for students	-.463	.384	.581	.264	1.044*	.006*
Teachers interest & acceptance	-.068	.986	.441	.585	.509	.423
Total	.014	1.000	1.572	.247	1.558	.191

*. The mean difference is significant at the 0.05 level

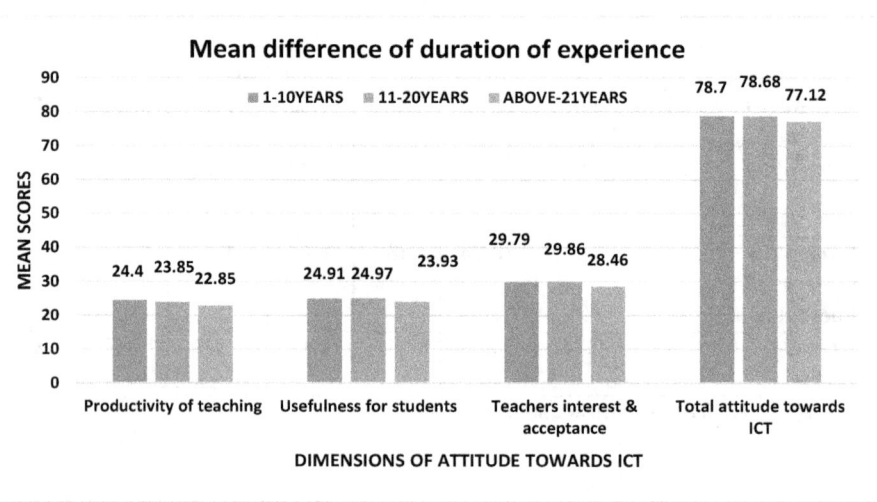

Fig.4.12 (B): Graphical representation of attitude towards ICT based on experience

Interpretation:

The F value from the given **ANOVA Table 4.12(B)** is1.847, p=.159, which found to be not significant at 0.05 level. It indicates that there is no significant difference in the total attitude towards ICT comprising three dimensions of college teachers about the length of experience. Tuckey's post hoc test in table **4.12.B (1)** identified honestly no significant difference among the total groups of the duration of experience of college teachers. So, the hypothesis, **(Ho12)** is accepted. The mean score of overall 1-10, 11-20 and above 21 years of experience teachers' falls within moderate favourable attitude level i.e. 78.70, 78.68and77.12 **(mentioned in Table 3.19).**

The significant difference is noticed in the **(usefulness for students' dimensions)** among 11-20 and above 21 years of experience. It is notable from the **ANOVA** table that the mean value of 1-10 and 10-20 years of experience is almost the same, but the mean value becomes less among above 21 years of experience. This is because, with the increase in age, adaptation to new technology becomes less feasible **Guo, Dobson, & Petrina (2008); Helsper & Eynon (2010).**

Teachers may find the use of technology in education to be time-consuming, confusing, and frustrating. Teachers with traditional beliefs are less likely to use computers as advocated **Ertmer (2005).** During the interview and field notes, it came into light that teacher-educators has a positive attitude towards the ICT and levels of technology usage in teacher education process but due to many problems faced by educators they were not employing ICT in teacher education process. If ICT-training, resources of ICTs, motivation, support of management and technical support besides benefits of ICT in education process acquainted to the teacher-educators then they can integrate ICT in teacher education process efficiently. **Madhavi and Vimala (2011)** infer from their study that employees in the age group of above 20 years conflicting demand with quality of work and eventually leave little time for them to go for technological innovation and have a lack of interest in adopting and accepting IT in the educational setup.

Tuckey's post hoc test result also exhibited significant differences among (11 – 20) and (above 21years) work experience in the dimensions of **(usefulness for students')**. The feasible reason is that the younger teachers were technically more advanced in teaching with better computer awareness and adequate skill than the rest of the age groups. Fewer experienced teachers have an explicit attitude to facilitate new technological knowledge effectively for the benefit of students in contrast to more experienced colleagues. Although, the senior teachers are well acquainted with academic productivity and also they have an interest in technology; they confronted the lack of training facilities to assimilate computer technology.

The present result is supported by **Onasanya, Shehu, Oduwaiye & Shehu (2010)** amazing result found that the less experienced lecturers were more engaging in the new confrontation of using ICT facilities than the senior ones. **Angadi (2014)** also examined that type of experience has no significant impact on the implementation of ICT among B.Ed. College teachers affiliated to Rani Channamma University Karnataka State.

Objective No. 13) To find out whether there is any relationship between the teaching effectiveness and the perception of organizational climate of college teachers.

(Ho13) There will be no significant relationship between teaching effectiveness and the perception of organizational climate of college teachers.

Table 4.13 (A): Correlation between teaching effectiveness and the perception of organizational climate in respect to gender, locality and duration of experience

Sl. No		Demographic Profile	Pearson Correlation between TES and OCQ
A	Total		.151**
B	Gender	Male	.078
C		Female	.212**
D	Area	Rural	.071
E		Urban	.339**
F	Experience (years)	Experience (1 – 10)	.193*
G		(11 – 20)	.139*
H		(above-21)	.141

**Correlation is significant at the 0.01 level (2-tailed)
* Correlation is significant at the 0.05 level (2-tailed)

In **Table 4.13(A),** the overall result interacts that there is a positive and significant correlation between teaching effectiveness and the perception of organizational climate concerning gender, locality, and duration of the experience. So, the hypothesis, (Ho12) is accepted. This means that a modest climate setting can strongly influence their effectiveness.

Table 4.13 (B): Pearson Correlations between teaching effectiveness & the perception of organizational climate

TES Dimensions	Phy. Env.	Library facility	Reward system	Relationship-colleagues	Support system	Acad. climate	Total OCQ
Academic and professional knowledge	.003	.096*	.038	.063	.033	.085*	.007
Preparation & presentation of lesson plan,	.067	.208**	.144**	.232**	.123**	.087*	.213**

classroom management								
Attitude towards students, parents, colleagues, head of institution	.084	.016	.171	.107*	.068	.151**	.090*	
Use of motivation reward, punishment & interest in all round development of students	.154**	.108*	.109*	.165**	.124**	.052	.114**	
Result, feedback accountability	.077	-.014	-.069	-.056	-.044	.097*	-.060	
Personal qualities	.051	-.065	.127**	.137**	.037	.094*	.119**	
TES-Total	.091*	.161**	.114**	.180**	.107*	.053	.151**	

* Correlation is significant at the 0.05 level (2-tailed).

** Correlation is significant at the 0.01 level (2-tailed).

From the above **Table 4.13(B)** it is observed that there is a positive significant correlation between total teaching effectiveness and all dimensions of the perception of organizational climate. So, the hypothesis (**Ho13**) is rejected. The correlation coefficient values of **academic and professional knowledge** are positively correlated with all dimensions of organizational climate. But specifically, **academic and professional knowledge** significantly associated with **library facilities (.096*) and academic climate (.085*).** That means adequate sitting arrangement, availability of different books in the library, proper existence of sufficient teaching aids, equal maintenance of fix schedule for class, can contribute to enhancing professional knowledge. Moreover, provisions for excursions related to various contents of subjects, active involvement of co-curricular activities with students also greatly impact on the academic efficiency of teachers.

Preparation & presentation of lesson plan, classroom management positively and significantly correlated with **physical environment (.067) library facilities (r=.208**) reward system (r=.144**) relationship with colleagues (.232**) support system(r=.123**) and academic climate (r=.087)** of organizational climate. This is because required infrastructure facilities, visual resources, library facilities to facilitate effective teaching, work-oriented time management, and full acquaintance of teaching objectives may foster teachers to deal effectively in teaching. In an organization with a high extent of teachers' punctuality, proper knowledge of educational psychology, collegiality, and participation, the teaching effectiveness is high, making the success of education higher as well.

Attitude towards students, parents, colleagues, and head of institution dimensions has a positive significant relationship with **reward system (.171**) relationship with colleagues (.107*) and academic climate (.151**)**. It means that sufficient cardinal bonding, decisions are taken effectively, organizing co-curricular activities and stimulation to create motivational opportunities, the practice of career development, and good remuneration system is believed to bring impact on the performance of the employee. The teachers and their heads must share a relationship based on equality and mutual respect to create a better and positive organizational climate.

A significant positive correlation also exists between the **use of motivation reward, punishment & interest in the all-round development of students** and all dimensions of organizational climate. The favourable physical environment has a significant positive effect on the efficiency of teachers. Environment facilities like cleanliness and other well- maintained facilities such as proper utilization of technological applications, teachers' competent usability of material aids may influence the overall aspects of the development of students. Supports system of organizational climate like provisions for teachers to participate in refreshers courses, funding for organizing seminars, workshops, etc. may automatically make benefaction for educational effectiveness. For complete integration of personality and efficient academic climate may signify an important role. The present-day curriculum helps in enhancing the learning process by designing extra-curricular activities merged with the academic climate. This may contribute to bringing social skills, moral values and other spheres of classroom affairs. It has suggested that if there is an increase in organizational climate, and then there will be an increase in teaching effectiveness.

The **result, feedback accountability** dimensions have a positive and significant relationship with the **physical environment (.077) and academic climate (.094*)** of the organization. The importance of the perception of organizational climate to teachers' effectiveness is a significant one. The Discussion may immerge that the physiological ambience of the organization influences the classroom teaching outcomes. It also evaluates that the teachers' feedback regarding the performance of students, conduction of periodical tests, assessment techniques are very much manipulated by the academic atmosphere of the organization. Moreover, **result, feedback accountability** negatively correlated with the **library facilities, rewards system, relationships with colleagues and support system of the organization.** That means that recognition of good work, professional jealousy of the staff members, and lack of building facilities, insufficient cordial relationship with colleagues may not hamper the assessment and appraisal of college teachers.

Personal qualities of teachers are strongly and positively correlated with the **physical environment (.051), rewards system (.127**), relationship with colleagues (.137**) and academic climate (.094*)** of the organization. This means that responsible and creative teachers can forward need-based subject-matter for the students; they are confident enough and have adjustment capacity. So, teachers with personal qualities may promote professional abilities, valued friendship within co-workers. Reward systems such as promotion given based on merit, proper recognition of good work done by the teachers, adequate feedback from other staff for their performance influence greatly on the effectiveness of college teachers. In such a case, the workplace can be attractive and people work beyond their duties and roles within the organization.

The study supported by **Selamat, Samsu & Kamalu (2013)** who revealed the organisational climate as a predominant factor that greatly impacts teachers' job performance. **Raza (2010), Katoch (2017)** determined a significant relationship between the perception of organizational climate and performance of college teachers teaching in degree colleges.

Objective No. 14) To investigate the correlation between teaching effectiveness and mental health of college teachers.

(Ho14) There will be no significant relationship between teaching effectiveness and mental health of college teachers.

Table 4.14 (A): Correlation between teaching effectiveness and mental health on the basis of gender, locality and duration of experience

Sl. No		Demographic Profile	Pearson Correlation between TES and EMHI
A	Total		.562**
B	Gender	Male	.528**
C		Female	.608**
D	Area	Rural	.559**
E		Urban	.447**
F	Experience (years)	Experience (1 – 10)	.664**
G		(11 – 20)	.536**
H		(21 – and above)	.495**

It is mentioned in the above **Table 4.14(A)** that there is a positive significant correlation between teaching effectiveness and the perception of organizational climate based on gender, locality, and duration of the experience. This means that the high-level mental health of college teachers instigates a higher level of teaching effectiveness. Simultaneously, modest mental detonation may also influence their effectiveness.

Table 4.14 (B): Pearson correlations between teaching effectiveness & mental health

DIMENSIONS OF TEACHING EFFECTIVENESS	TOTAL MENTAL HEALTH SCORES
Academic &professional knowledge	.391**
Preparation &presentation of lesson plan, classroom management	.522**

Attitude towards students, parents, colleagues, head of institution	.550**
Use of motivation reward, punishment & interest in all round development of students	.532**
Result, feedback accountability	.358**
Personal qualities	.458**
TES-Total	.562**

**Correlation is significant at the 0.01 level (2-tailed).

From the above **Table 4.14(B)** it is observed that there is a significant positive correlation between mental health and teaching effectiveness in all the six areas. So, the hypothesis (**Ho 14**) is rejected. Mental health has a vital role in teaching effectiveness in all areas. Results indicate that teachers with mentally competent have a high level of teaching effectiveness. This is because good mental health is the prerequisites for a good and effective teacher. Healthy and mentally competent teachers can contribute in the field of teaching with great enthusiasm; make effective use of material aids, pay individual attention to each student, can make efforts to introduce new methods and techniques in teaching, which greatly influence the effectiveness of teachers.

Similar results propounded by **Goel (2011), Devi & Talukdar (2018), Sethi (2015)** highlighted a significant positive relationship between mental health and teaching effectiveness of college teachers.

Objective No.15) To investigate the relationship between teaching effectiveness of college teachers and their attitude towards ICT.

(Ho15) There will be no significant relationship between teaching effectiveness and attitude towards ICT of college teachers.

Table 4.15 (A): Correlation between teaching effectiveness and attitude towards ICT based on gender, locality and duration of experience

Sl. No		Demographic Profile	Pearson Correlation between TES and ATICT
A	Total		.140**
B	Gender	Male	.006
C		Female	.247**
D	Area	Rural	.190**
E		Urban	.089
F	Experience (years)	Experience (1 – 10)	.143
G		(11 – 20)	.188*
H		(21 – and above)	.102

The above **Table 4.15(A)** identify that there is an overall significant and positive correlation between teaching effectiveness and attitude towards ICT based on gender, locality, and duration of the experience. But, in respect of female college teachers, rural areas teachers and teachers with 11-20 years of teaching experience have their significant positive correlation between teaching effectiveness and attitude towards ICT. That means that their teaching effectiveness is very much influenced by the positive attitude towards ICT.

Table 4.15 (B): Pearson correlations between teaching effectiveness and attitude towards ICT

DIMENSIONS OF TEACHING EFFECTIVENESS	DIMENSIONS OF ATTITUDE TOWARDS ICT			
	Productivity of teaching	Usefulness for students	Teachers interest and acceptance	Total attitude
Academic &professional knowledge	.073	.053	.013	.059

Preparation &presentation of lesson plan, classroom management	.098*	.115**	.090*	.129**
Attitude towards students, parents, colleagues, head of institution	.107*	.096*	.108*	.134**
Use of motivation reward, punishment & interest in all round development of students	.119**	.098*	.054	.116**
Result, feedback accountability	.101*	.128**	.090*	.135**
Personal qualities	.106*	.093*	.108*	.132**
TES-Total	.115**	.113**	.098*	.140**

**Correlation is significant at the 0.01 level (2-tailed).

*Correlation is significant at the 0.05 level (2-tailed).

The above **Table 4.15(B)** there exists a positive and significant relationship between total teaching effectiveness and total attitude towards ICT of college teachers. So, the hypothesis (Ho15) is rejected. A positive but not significant relationship is there in **academic & professional knowledge** with all three areas of attitude towards ICT i.e. **productivity of teaching (.073), usefulness for students (.053) and teachers' interest and acceptance (.013)** of college teachers. **Preparation & presentation of the lesson plan, classroom management** has a positive and significant relationship with the productivity of teaching (.098*), usefulness for students (.115**) and teachers' interest and acceptance (.090*). It means that attitude towards information technology has a significant role to play in deciding the teaching effectiveness of college teachers. They believe that information technology improves the quality of teaching and also provides knowledge and application package for teaching in the classroom. Most of the teachers believe in the educational values of information technology. From the response sheet, it also found that most of the college teachers can apply technology in classes which preferably improve the professional advancement and development of lecturers. Several studies have revealed that ICT-related training programs develop teachers' competences in computer use **Bauer & Kenton (2005); Franklin (2007).**

Attitude towards students, parents, colleagues, head of the institution of college teachers significantly and positively correlated with the **productivity of teaching (.107*), usefulness for students (.096*) and teachers' interest and acceptance (.108*).** This means that information technology provides fast and efficient means of getting the relevant information through the internet which enhances motivational opportunities in teaching practices. The positive attitude of teachers towards technology may facilitate teachers' in the acquisition of basic technological skills with the help of co-operative efforts. The result indicates that most of the college teachers may have sufficient computer literacy. It is noteworthy that information technology may increase the confidence level of teachers to find the solution for educational problems.

Use of motivation reward, punishment & interest in the all-round development of students, dimensions of teaching effectiveness caries positive and significant correlation with the **productivity of teaching (.119**) and usefulness of students (.098*).** This means that a positive attitude towards ICT provides remedial measures and productive use of material aids which may contribute to new teaching practices among teachers. The use of technology in education contributes a lot to the pedagogical aspects in which the application of ICT will lead to effective learning with the help and supports of ICT elements and components **(Jamieson-Proctor et al., 2007)**. The response sheet inculcates that a positive attitude towards ICT in teaching will enhance the learning process and maximizes the students' abilities in active learning. The previous studies of **(Finger & Trinidad, 2002; Jorge et al., 2003; Young, 2003; Jamieson-Procter et al., 2013)** assists a positive relationship of attitude towards ICT with all-round development of students.

Teaching effectiveness dimensions i.e. **Result, feedback accountability** also has a positive and significant relationship with all three areas of attitude towards ICT namely **productivity of teaching (.101*), usefulness for students (.128*) and teachers interest and acceptance (.090*).** In teaching, affairs communication plays a pivot role and in this respect, ICT application is more preferable than ordinary posts. Technology-based teaching and learning offer various interesting ways which include educational videos, stimulation, storage of data, and the usage of databases that will make the learning process more fulfilling and meaningful. The current result indicates that a teacher's **interest and acceptance is strongly assimilated with teaching effectiveness.** Supporting this point **Winzenried, Dalgarno & Tinkler (2010)** fount that teachers who have gone through the ICT course are more effective in teaching by using technology tools.

Similarly, the **personal qualities** dimensions of teaching effectiveness are also significantly related to **the productivity of teaching (.106*), usefulness for students (.093*) and teachers' interest and acceptance (.108*).** This signifies that the integration of ICT is mostly dependent on the personal factors which define as self-perceptions. As ICT in education refers to the use of computer-based communication that incorporates into a daily classroom instructional process that needs an energetic, humorous and enthusiastic employee. This implies that the affirmative attitude of the technological aspects of college teachers may have an impact on overall teaching effectiveness.

Rajeswari & Sree (2017); Ruth Oluwatosin Adeyemo, Emmanuel Olusola Adu & Olusesan Adeyemi Adelabu (2015) indicated the application of technology as an instrument of effective teaching and learning.

Objective No. 16) To study the relationship between the perception of organizational climate and mental health of college teachers.

(Ho16) There will be no significant relationship between the perception of organizational climate and mental health of college teachers.

Table4.16 (A): Correlation between the perception of organizational climate and mental health based on gender, locality and duration of experience

Sl. No		Demographic Profile	Pearson Correlation between OCQ and EMHI
A	Total		.192**
B	Gender	Male	.182**
C		Female	.118
D	Area	Rural	.282**
E		Urban	.143*
F	Experience (years)	Experience (1 – 10)	.385**
G		(11 – 20)	.177*
H		(21 – and above)	.197**

* Correlation is significant at the 0.05 level (2-tailed).
** Correlation is significant at the 0.01 level (2-tailed).

The above **Table 4.16(A)** identify that there is an overall significant and positive correlation between the perception of organizational climate and mental health based on gender, locality, and duration of the experience. That means teachers with positive favourable climate have a higher level of mental health conditions. On the contrary, teachers with a moderate favourable climate instigate average mental health status. So, in the case of college teachers, their mental health status slightly depends on a positive perception of organizational climate.

Table 4.16 (B): Pearson correlations between the perception of organizational climate and mental health

DIMENSIONS OF ORGANIZATIONAL CLIMATE	TOTAL EMPLOYEES MENTAL HEALTH
Physical environment	.167**
Library facilities	.197**
Reward system	.170**
Relationship with colleagues	.277**
Support system	.120**
Academic climate	.072
Total-OCQ	.192**

**Correlation is significant at the 0.01 level (2-tailed).

Table 4.16(B) indicates a significant positive relationship between total mental health and the perception of organizational climate dimensions of the **physical environment (.167**), relationship with colleagues (.277**), support system (.120**) and academic climate (.072).** So, the hypothesis, (Ho16) is rejected. This means that teachers who experienced healthy mental health at work may be due to affirmative physical conditions. Studies propounded by **Helbich (2018)** also support the point that friendly environmental exposures, especially sufficient air quality, noise, ergonomic conditions, and housing conditions, may accurately affect workers' mental health. Encouraging organizational settings may improve employees' self-accepting behaviour, may inculcate with the adequacy to manage varied aspects like communication skills, decision making, stimulating a supportive atmosphere among co-workers, etc. There is also an important influence of mental health on academic climate as health professionals may promote higher academic achievement.

The study supported by **Gondlekar & Kamat (2016)** who have clearly mentioned that employee's positive perception of their organization ultimately impacting their overall mental health status. **Pan & Wu (2015); Bronkhorst, Tummers, Steijn & Vijverberg (2014)** also clearly investigated that teachers' mental health was affected by the perception of organizational climate in university.

Objective No. 17) To find out whether there is any relationship between the perception of organizational climate and attitude towards ICT of college teachers.

(Ho17) There will be no significant relationship between the perception of organizational climate and attitude towards ICT of college teachers.

Table 4.17 (A): Correlation between the perception of organizational climate and attitude towards ICT based on gender, locality and duration of experience

Sl. No		Demographic Profile	Pearson Correlation between OCQ and ATICT
A	Total		.032
B	Gender	Male	.017
C		Female	.044
D	Area	Rural	.002
E		Urban	.071
F	Experience (years)	Experience (1 – 10)	.137
G		(11 – 20)	.084
H		(21 – and above)	.072

The above **Table 4.17(A)** describes positive but not significant correlation between the perception of organizational climate and attitude towards ICT based on gender, locality and duration of experience. That means teachers belonging to both highly /moderate favourable climate may proceed to acquire a satisfactory/average level of attitude towards ICT.

Table 4.17 (B): Pearson correlations between the perception of organizational climate and attitude towards ICT

AREAS	Productivity of teaching	Usefulness for students	Teachers interest and acceptance	Total attitude
Physical environment	.061	.033	.007	.012
Library facilities	.120**	.030	.007	.046
Reward system	.049	.063	.053	.070
Relationship with colleagues	-.006	-.017	-.054	-.034
Support system	.020	.036	.142**	.087*
Academic climate	.038	.006	.087	.020
OCQ-Total	.013	.022	.040	.032

* Correlation is significant at the 0.05 level (2-tailed).
** Correlation is significant at the 0.01 level (2-tailed).

Table 4.17(B) signifies a positive but not significant overall relationship between the perception of organizational climate dimensions of the **physical environment** and three areas of attitude towards ICT i.e. **productivity of teaching (.061), the usefulness of students (.033) and teachers' interest and acceptance (.012)**. So, the hypothesis Ho17) is accepted. The reason is that proper facilities of the skilful use of technology when linked to pedagogical strategies may worthwhile the optimistic attitude towards ICT implementation. It may also motivate teachers to learn the use of IT devices in teaching which may lead to demand professional advancement.

The **library facilities** of the organization have a positive and significant relationship with the **productivity of teaching (.120**)**. It also has an only positive but not significant relationship with the **usefulness of students (.030) and teachers' interest and acceptance (.007).** This means that library building fully equipped with e-library resources especially e-journals, CD-ROM databases, online databases, web-based resources and a variety of other electronic resources may significantly provide necessary instructional aids for teachers. This may facilitate teachers for the acquisition of efficient means of information in teaching. This results also supported by **Abdullahi (2013).**

The **reward system** of the organization is positively correlated with the attitude towards ICT areas like the **productivity of teaching (.049), the usefulness of students (.063) and teachers' interest and acceptance (.053).** The organizations' reward system is one such copious account that influences the constructive attitude concerning technological knowledge. Teachers with positive vibes about their work are more likely to persevere in their search for new and varied technologies, and therefore, have a greater tendency to perform better in terms of intellectual achievements. Proper recognition of the abilities of teachers' usability of technology within the ethical limits may have a positive impact on technology implication. In a similar vein, researchers in the technology domain have observed the positive relationship between a supportive reward system and motivation of technologists in information technology **(Sankar, Ledbetter, Snyder, Roberts, McCreary & Boyles, 1991).** Reward systems such as promotion given based on new technology innovation, identification of good work done by the teachers may influence greatly the positive attitude towards the application of ICT.

Another dimension of organization i.e. **relationship with colleagues** carries negative but not significant interaction with all the three areas of attitude towards ICT, such as productivity of **teaching (-.006), the usefulness of students (-.017) and teachers'** interest and acceptance (-.054). This indicates that the professional jealousy, insufficient cordial relationship with colleagues cannot hamper the professional responsibilities of college teachers.

The **support system** and **academic climate** of the organization also positively correlated accordingly with **productivity of teaching (.020, .038), the usefulness of students (.036, .006) and teachers' interest and acceptance (.142**, .087) dimensions of attitude towards ICT.** This interprets that financial and infrastructural organization resources, technology-based training, personal and organisational relationships, staff coordination and upliftment, administrative support, the pressure to use technology, all may have a guarantee with positive outcomes of introducing new technology. Additionally, facilitating tools and technology was positively associated with high levels of perceived behavioural control towards knowledge sharing. Research conducted by **Wepner, Tao, & Ziomek (2006)** also support that teachers who are committed to professional development activities gain knowledge of ICT integration and classroom technology organization.

The result is consistent with the study **Karanja (2016)** which does not indicate any significant relationship between organizational climates, technological innovation among employees. **Yoo, Huang & Lee (2012)** who exhibit a canonical positive correlation between employees' perceived organizational climate and their acceptance levels toward e-learning. **Dawoud (2010)** also provides a better understanding of the positive relationship between the perception of organizational climate and information communication technology.

Objective No. 18) To find out the correlation between mental health and attitude towards ICT of college teachers.

(Ho18) There will be no significant relationship between mental health and attitude towards ICT of college teachers.

Table 4.18 (A): Correlation between mental health and attitude towards ICT based on gender, locality and duration of experience

Sl. No		Demographic Profile	Pearson Correlation between EMHI and ATICT
A	Total		.024
B	Gender	Male	.031
C		Female	.065
D	Area	Rural	.006
E		Urban	.016
F	Experience (years)	Experience (1 – 10)	.038
G		(11 – 20)	.068
H		(21 – and above)	.017

The above **Table 4.18(A)** describes positive but not significant correlation between the perception of organizational climate and attitude towards ICT in respect to gender, locality and duration of experience. This mentions that college teachers with a highly favourable mental health status have strongly influenced the favourable attitude towards ICT.

Table 4.18 (B): Pearson correlations between mental health and attitude towards ICT

DIMENSIONS OF ATTITUDE TOWARDS ICT	TOTAL EMPLOYEES MENTAL HEALTH
Productivity of teaching	.062
Usefulness for students	.013
Teachers interest and acceptance	.002

Table 4.18(B) signifies a positive but not significant relationship between mental health and all three areas of attitude towards ICT i.e. **productivity of teaching (.062), the usefulness of students (.013) and teachers' interest and acceptance (.002).** So, the hypothesis, (Ho18) is accepted. It meant that if there is an increase/decrease in mental health then there would be an increase/decrease in attitude towards ICT. Hence, good mental health can instigate teachers to adopt technology in a productive way. Technology application can reduce the workload which generally reduces tensions and mental fatigue during teaching practices and this may lead to positive mental health outcomes. Reversely, sound physiological health including wellbeing, satisfaction, adjustment, creativity, ability to enjoy, social support and such may help teachers to take up positively with the new trends of technology. From the response sheet, it also observed that the employee who are free from psyche-physiological distress can adequately emancipate with the computer-assisted instruction. Moreover, college teachers generally have academic pressure of work. So, positive attitude technological prospects can enhance work productivity. In other words, this finding proves that activities related to technical equipment can lessen the insufficient study time, academic burden of work which can be influential in producing healthy physiological health.

The study is similar with **Forsman & Nordmyr (2017)** who examined an overall positive association between Internet use and mental health and its psychosocial covariates. **Beckhoff, Nielsen & Larsen (2018)** also put emphasize towards a solid knowledge based on the significant association between positive computer technology attitude and mental health.

4.19. *Multiple Regression Analysis:*

Table 4.19 (a): Model summary

Model	R	R Square	Adjusted R Square	Std. Error of the Estimate
1	.578a	.334	.330	23.103

a. Predictors: (Constant), TOT_OCQ, Tot EMHI, Tot_Attitude

Table 4.19 (b): F-ratio

Model	Sum of squares	df	Mean square	F	Sig.
Regression	144340.792	3	48113.597	90.141	.00a
Residual	288229.898	540	533.759		
Total	432570.689	543			

a. Dependent Variable: TES_Total

Table 4.19 (c): The Estimate model Coefficients

Model	Unstandardized Coefficients		Standardized Coefficients	t	Sig.
	B	Std. Error	Beta		
Constant	250.765	14.030		17.873	.000
Total organizational climate	.118	.103	.041	4.143	.000
Total employees mental health	3.864	.251	.551	15.403	.000
Total attitude towards ICT	.400	.113	.125	3.553	.000

The above **Table 4.19(a)** represented the Model Summary indicating three Predictors (OCQ, EMHI, ATTITUDE) of the model, where multiple correlation coefficient(R) of TES with OCQ, EMHI, ATTITUDE among college teachers was found to be R=0.578, further R Square Change =0.334 which represents the actual contribution of TES on OCQ, EMHI, ATTITUDE, the real covariance magnitude of Predictor variables: OCQ,

EMHI, ATTITUDE contribute to the criterion variable: TES came out as 33.4%. Multiple correlation coefficient(R) can be considered to be one measure of the quality of the prediction of the criterion variable. In this study, value of 0.578 indicates a moderate level of prediction.

The F-ratio in the **ANOVA** table **[Table 4.19(b)]** shows whether the overall regression model is a good fit for the data. The table shows that the predictor variables statistically significantly predict the criterion variable, $F = 90.141$, $p <.0001$ (i.e. the regression model is a good fit of the data).

Table 4.19(c) (coefficient) indicated that **OCQ, EMHI, ATTITUDE** (predictors) influences TES (criterion) among college teachers. The Statistical value given in the mentioned table indicated that values for $t = 4.143$ (**OCQ**); t value 15.403 (**EMHI**) and 3.553 (**ATTITUDE**) are significant and also show the positive relationship between **OCQ, EMHI, ATTITUDE** and TES. Based on these finding it can be concluded that **OCQ, EMHI, ATTITUDE** has its positive and significant relationship with teaching effectiveness of the college teachers.

The finding of the present study is consistent with previous research studies. Organizational climate, attitudes towards using new technology have been shown a significant correlation with the teaching effectiveness of college teachers. As reported by some researches, teachers who expressed high levels of effectiveness in teaching with favourable mental health were motivated to participate in relevant organizational activities. That means teaching effectiveness is very much influenced by the perception of organizational climate and mental health condition (**Babu & Kumari, 2013; Selamat, Samsu & Kamalu, 2013; Riti, 2010; Goel, 2011; Bronkhorst,**

Tummers, Steijn & Vijverberg, 2014). In a similar way, most of the teachers showed better performance rated to open climate. Likewise, some instigators also indicated the importance of teaching competence to inculcate the attitude towards ICT of teacher educators **(Islahi, 2010; Rajeswari & Sree, 2017).**

4.20 *Hypotheses Verification:*

(Ho1) There will be no significant difference in teaching effectiveness of male and female college teachers- **A**ccepted.

(Ho2) There will be no significant difference of locality (rural/urban) on teaching effectiveness of college teachers- **N**ot accepted.

(Ho3) There will be no significant difference in duration of experience on teaching effectiveness of college teachers- **A**ccepted.

(Ho4) There will be no significant difference in the perception of organizational climate of male and female college teachers- **N**ot accepted.

(Ho5) There will be no significant difference in the perception of organizational climate of rural and urban college teachers- **N**ot accepted.

(Ho6) There will be no significant difference in the perception of organizational climate of college teachers based on the duration of experience- **A**ccepted.

(Ho7) There will be no significant difference in the mental health of male and female college teachers- **N**ot accepted.

(Ho8) There will be no significant difference in the mental health of rural and urban college teachers- **N**ot accepted.

(Ho9): There will be no significant difference in the mental health of college teachers on the basis of duration of experience- **N**ot accepted.

(Ho10) There will be no significant difference in the attitude towards ICT of male and female college teachers- Accepted.

(Ho11) There will be no significant difference in the attitude towards ICT of rural and urban college teachers- Accepted.

(Ho12) There will be no significant difference in attitude towards ICT of college teachers on the basis of duration of experience- Accepted.

(Ho13) There will be no significant relationship between teaching effectiveness and the perception of organizational climate of college teachers- Not accepted.

(Ho14) There will be no significant relationship between teaching effectiveness and mental health of college teachers- Not accepted.

(Ho15) There will be no significant relationship between teaching effectiveness and attitude towards ICT of college teachers- Not accepted.

(Ho16) There will be no significant relationship between the perception of organizational climate and mental health of college teachers- Not accepted.

(Ho17) There will be no significant relationship between the perception of organizational climate and attitude towards ICT of college teachers- accepted.

(Ho18) There will be no significant relationship between mental health and attitude towards ICT of college teachers- accepted.

4. 21. *An Overview of the Results*:

Analysis of the overall result depicts gender influences on the variables under study. Female students yielded a higher score on teaching effectiveness with different dimensions among the college teachers. They maintain better interpersonal social relationships, have clearer goals in life and have more flexibility as compared to the males. It is found that male teachers are more independent and able to cope effectively with a varied situation of the organizational climate. They are also competent enough to deal with stress management techniques. However, enough evidence is found for the influence of locality on the variables under study. Only urban areas teachers scored higher in their teaching effectiveness and mental health status than the teachers of rural areas. Results also revealed that urban-related college teachers perceived their organizational climate and mental health condition as better than rural areas. Findings also reveal the tremendous influence of teaching experience on the mental health and of college teachers. The teachers with increasing teaching experience may sometimes confront with difficulty in maintaining work-life balance. Although most of the college teachers have their positive favourable attitude regarding gender locality and teaching experience; still, the teachers above 21 years of experience are facing problems to implement the ICT innovations in teaching due to lack of knowledge and training facilities to assimilate computer technology. Also, a positive correlation is found between teaching effectiveness, organizational climate, mental health and attitude towards ICT of college teachers. It is found that perceived organizational climate and mental health significantly associated with the effectiveness of teaching of college teachers. The majority of both rural and urban college teachers who experienced a moderate level of organizational climate and mental health had a significant influence on the attitude towards ICT application.

CHAPTER: 5
SUMMARY, FINDINGS AND SUGGESTIONS

5.1 SUMMARY AND FINDINGS:

Research has suggested that every educational institution is considered to be the scaffold, based on which, the task of producing effective citizens is the principal responsibility of the educational system can emerge. The explosion of the area of knowledge, the convergence of digital technologies and knowledge, globalization acts as a prime factor in the emerging society. The youth of today hence, are experiencing towards the millennium of a complete challenge to cope up with the new developments. So, these trends in society demand subsequent changes in the education system. To initiate desirable learning outcomes, the teacher plays a responsible role in providing knowledge to equip and acquire a vision for sustainable development. The whole educational system is immobilized in the absenteeism of excellent and effective teachers. The present study will explore the correlates of teacher effectiveness. Once the correlates are found, the steps can be taken to bring improvements in classroom teaching. The existing fact is that the climate or environment is the kernel of any institution. All the members of an institution or an organization are being influenced by its climate because there are many factors in the climate which influence the proper growth and development of an individual. It will affect the teacher's performance as well. The study is confined to the degree college teachers as the qualitative transition of the whole educational system is supported by the efficiency of teachers. Aside from their academic requirements, college teachers also have different responsibilities brought about by their different life roles. Based on the above discussion it is said that the teaching is largely a dual allegiance possession in which teacher function covers both within the classroom and also an active member with the whole of the organization. That means the areas of teaching take place in different emphasizes on the organisation, school administration, teacher effectiveness, and socio-personal interaction. In this context, the present researcher had laid her attention to the question of whether the present system of college climate and teaching effectiveness was fruitful or not. Present-day challenging and over whelming roles of twenty-first-century teachers may lead to high levels of stress, emotional imbalances and maladjustment with the job. Although they have some challenging lifestyles, they still have some mental assets within themselves which help to sustain in this competitive world. The behaviour of teachers towards these situations is important which is governed by the psycho-physiological and personal factors. Therefore, the investigator made a humble attempt to make a review of the studies done in the field of teaching effectiveness and also try to determine the interaction of the perception of organizational climate and mental health with it. To attain all-round achievement one needs to preservation new collection and dissemination of knowledge in a convenient manner. With the help of new technology now teachers are exploring new ideas for teaching and learning. Likewise, technology plays a crucial role in this regard. These tools are also making the teaching-learning process very interesting and conducive. **Huang & Liaw (2005)** explored that teachers with a positive outlook towards the use of educational technology act as a weapon to provide useful insight into the integration of ICT into teaching processes. Competition for academic upliftment and expectation for better results are openly noticeable in most of the college teachers. Teachers who are working in college around Guwahati are no exception to it. So, the researcher planned to explore the association between teacher effectiveness, organizational climate, mental health and the attitude toward the ICT among college teachers of Kamrup district, Assam. It is also noteworthy to state that the current research was carried out in an unidentified area in the Indian context.

Thus, the study primarily attempted to answer two research questions. These are as follows:

3. Is there any relationship that exists between teaching effectiveness, organizational climate, mental health and attitude towards ICT?
4. Do teaching effectiveness, organizational climate, mental health and attitude towards ICT differ with gender, locality, and duration of experience?

To investigate these research questions, the main aim of the present study was envisaged to assess the correlation between teaching effectiveness, organizational climate, mental health and attitude towards ICT of college teachers based on (i) Gender (ii) Locality and (iii) Duration of experience.

In the present study the following objectives were formulated for verification:

- To find out and compare the teaching effectiveness of male and female college teachers.
- To find out and compare the teaching effectiveness of rural and urban college teachers.
- To find out and compare the teaching effectiveness of three groups of teaching experience (1-10 years, 11-20 years and above 21 years) among college teachers.
- To find out and compare the perception of organizational climate of male and female college, teachers

- To find out and compare the perception of organizational climate of rural and urban college teachers.
- To find out and compare the perception of organizational climate of college teachers regarding the duration of the experience (1-10, 11-20 and above 21 years).
- To find out and compare the mental health of male and female college teachers.
- To find out and compare the mental health of rural and urban college teachers.
- To find out and compare the mental health of college teachers based on the duration of the experience (1-10, 11-20 and above 21 years).
- To find out and compare the level of attitude towards ICT of male and female college teachers.
- To find out and compare the level of attitude towards ICT of rural and urban college teachers.
- To find out and compare the level of attitude towards ICT of college teachers based on the duration of the experience (1-10, 11-20 and above 21 years).
- To investigate the relationship between the teaching effectiveness and perception of organizational climate of college teachers.
- To study the correlation between teaching effectiveness and mental health of college teachers.
- To study the relationship between the teaching effectiveness of college teachers and their attitude towards ICT.
- To find out the correlation between the perception of organizational climate and mental health of college teachers.

- To find out the relationship between the perception of organizational climate and attitude towards ICT of college teachers.
- To find out the correlation between mental health and attitude towards ICT among college teachers.

Accordingly, the following **hypotheses** were formulated-

Taking into account the literature available comprising the independent variables of the study, some null hypothesis are framed for empirical verifications. To test the significance of difference, the null hypothesis is a useful technique. Because it is better to think no differences exist between the two variables until it is proved scientifically. In the present study, the researcher wants to check if there is any differences exist, so the researcher decided to formulate the null hypothesis. The following are the null hypothesis formulated to test the tenability of the hypothesis.

Ho1) There will be no significant difference in teaching effectiveness of male and female college teachers.

Ho2) There will be no significant difference in teaching effectiveness of rural and urban college teachers.

Ho3) There will be no significant difference in the duration of the experience (1-10, 11-20 and above 21 years) on teaching effectiveness of college teachers.

Ho4) There will be no significant difference in the perception of organizational climate of gender (male/female) college teachers.

Ho5) There will be no significant difference in the perception of organizational climate of rural and urban college teachers.

Ho6) There will be no significant difference in the perception of organizational climate of college teachers regarding the duration of the experience (1-10, 11-20 and above 21 years).

Ho7) There will be no significant difference in the mental health of male and female college teachers.

Ho8) There will be no significant difference in the mental health of rural and urban college teachers.

Ho9) There will be no significant difference in the mental health of college teachers based on the duration of the experience (1-10, 11-20 and above 21 years).

Ho10) There will be no significant difference in the attitude towards ICT of male and female college teachers.

Ho11) There will be no significant difference in the attitude towards ICT of rural and urban college teachers.

Ho12) There will be no significant difference in the attitude towards ICT of college teachers concerning the duration of the experience (1-10, 11-20 and above 21 years).

Ho13) There will be no significant relationship between teaching effectiveness and the perception of organizational climate of college teachers.

Ho14) There will be no significant correlation between teaching effectiveness and the mental health of college teachers.

Ho15) There will be no significant correlation between teaching effectiveness and attitude towards ICT of college teachers.

Ho16) There will be no significant correlation between the perception of organizational climate and mental health of college teachers.

Ho17) There will be no significant correlation between the perception of organizational climate and attitude towards ICT of college teachers.

Ho18) There will be no significant relationship between mental health and attitude towards ICT of college teachers.

In the present study, the population refers to the college teachers working in reputed government degree colleges (included both B.A & B.Sc.) affiliated by Gauhati University of Kamrup District, Assam. To be recruited the sample, two sampling techniques, namely purposive Sampling and proportionate stratified random sampling technique were employed. The name of the educational institutions and departments were chosen with the help of purposive sampling technique and college teachers were selected with the help of proportionate stratified random sampling. In this study, **quantitative research methods** are utilized to test the proposed hypotheses. The sample consisted of –

- 274 male teachers and 274 female teachers= 548
- 274 rural teachers and 274 urban teachers= 548
- 153 teachers with 1-10 years, 223 teachers with 11-20 years and 172 teachers comprising above 21 years of experience= 548

The descriptive survey method of research was taken for the given study to collect data from the degree of college teachers. Since the present study attempted to correlate the findings and hence was used correlation design which told the bivariate relations between the variables. In this study, four variables were treated as key variables. These were: 'teaching effectiveness', 'organizational climate', 'mental health' and 'attitude towards ICT'. Among these variables teaching effectiveness, organizational climate, mental health and attitude towards ICT were dependent variable while the independent variables were gender (male/female), locality (rural/urban) & duration of experience (1-10 years, 11-20years & above 21 years).

The study was designed to assess the validity of the variables mentioned in the proposed model of teaching effectiveness. Very specifically, the investigator attempted to investigate whether and to what extent organizational climate, mental health and attitude towards ICT jointly and/or separately, either way possible, assist in predicting teaching effectiveness of college teachers. The investigator also tries to examine and compare each of the variables based on some independent variables among the college teachers working in degree colleges in Kamrup district, Assam.

The researcher used both the standardized tools namely *teacher effectiveness Scale*, comprising six different dimensions of teaching effectiveness namely- academic & professional knowledge, Preparation & presentation of lesson plan, classroom management, attitude towards students/ head of institution/ colleagues/parents, use of motivation reward/ punishment/interest in the all-round development of students, result, feedback accountability and personal qualities.

Likewise, the *Organizational climate* consists of 35 items on a 5 point Likert Scale which was constructed and standardized by the researcher with the guidance of her Research Supervisor and validated by the Experts. These statements were then categorized in terms of the several dimensions of organizational climate like, physical environment, library facilities, and reward system of the organization, relationship with colleagues, support System and academic climate.

Employees mental health inventory comprising of 24 items also used for the given study. Hence, a*ttitude towards ICT questionnaire* is self-devised with the guidance of experts and the supervisor was also applied for the study. In this scale, there were 24 items and against each item, five options were there. These items were of two kinds, that is, positive and negative and fell under six dimensions, namely: productivity of teaching, usefulness for students and teachers interest and acceptance.

After administering the tools for the entire sample, scoring was done following the manuals for the scales. The interpretations of the scores were done comparing the Norm tables of the scales. Data were statistically treated by using SPSS, Version: 16.0

The final results and interpretations of the data were collected in the following manner:

- Descriptive Statistical Analysis was calculated to study the variation of the score.
- The statistical test ANOVA was applied to find out a difference in groups of college teachers based on the duration of experience, followed by Tuckey's Test.
- Pearson product-moment correlation was used among the four variables.
- Multiple regression analysis was performed to test the contribution of organizational climate, mental health, and attitude towards ICT in predicting teaching effectiveness among college teachers.

After the statistical analysis, obtained results were presented in tabular form and graphical presentation followed by explanation and discussion.

5.2 *Findings of the study:*

After statistical analysis, the results were drawn and all the results were discussed appropriately which are listed below.

- No significant gender differences were identified in teaching effectiveness among college teachers. But the females yielded a higher mean score than the males in some aspects of teaching.

- The result indicated a prominent distinction in the variable 'teaching effectiveness' of college teachers based on locality. Urban college teacher's effectiveness found to be higher than the rural areas.
- Statistically no significant dissimilarity was noted in total teaching effectiveness concerning the duration of the experience. But it can be noticed that the mean score of 11-20 years inculcates a higher level of effectiveness than 1-10 and above 21 years of college teachers.
- The perception of organizational climate has a significant influence on the college teachers based on gender. Male teachers had a positively favourable perception towards institutional climate compared to the female college teachers.
- Statistically, a significant difference was seen in the perception of organizational climate of rural and urban college teachers. Urban related college teachers had a positively favourable perception of organizational climate than rural areas.
- The findings carried no significant statistical difference of college teacher's perception of organizational climate based on the duration of the experience. This means that 1-10, 11-20 and above 21 years of experience teachers had a moderate favourable perception of organizational climate at each level.
- There was a highly significant difference in the mental health of college teachers based on gender. Male college teachers had favourable mental health conditions than female teachers.
- The highly significant distinction was there in the mental health of college teachers based on locality. The urban college teachers faced with a highly favourable mental health status than rural teachers.

- The teaching experience of college teachers was found to be a significant influence on mental health. 1-10 years' experience teachers had indicated a high level of mental health in comparison to 11-20 and above 21 years' experience of college teachers.
- The results also put forward the non-significant variation between male and female college teachers concerning attitude towards ICT. Both genders had a moderately favourable attitude towards ICT.
- Statistically, no significant difference was found in attitude towards ICT awareness based on locality. But in respect of urban teachers, they had a positive favourable attitude towards ICT awareness than the rural college teachers.
- Statistically, no significant difference was found in the overall attitude towards ICT based on the duration of experience of college teachers. They had exposed a moderately favourable attitude towards ICT according to their level of teaching experience.
- A positive relation was seen between teaching effectiveness and the perception of organizational climate based on male/female, rural/urban, and duration of the experience. A positive favourable climate leads to a higher level of effectiveness. It was found that rural teachers with an average level of teaching effectiveness exhibited moderate perception of organizational climate conditions. In urban areas, favourable perception of organizational climate automatically enhanced teaching effectiveness of college teachers. Again, regarding the teaching experience of college teachers above 21 years who had confronted with moderate perception of organizational climate also contributed to average effectiveness in the teaching process of college teachers.

- Highly positive and also a significant relationship were found between total teaching effectiveness and all dimensions of the perception of organizational climate.
- There was a positive but also a significant correlation between teaching effectiveness and mental health based on gender, locality, and the duration of the experience. It also determined that male teachers with adequate mental and physiological health were contributing to a higher level of effectiveness. In rural areas, a medium level of mental health had influence lower level of effectiveness. But in urban areas satisfactory mental health conditions had led to higher efficiency in teaching. In the case of teaching experience, although 1-10 and 11-20 years of experience teachers had undergone a medium level of mental health, they were somehow managed competently in teaching practices. However, above 21 years' experience teachers with an average level of teaching effectiveness were very much motivated by the lower level of mental health.
- A significant and positive correlation was observed between the six areas of teaching effectiveness college teachers and their mental health.
- Positive and also significant relation was there between teaching effectiveness and attitude towards ICT of college teachers concerning male/female, rural/urban, and duration of the experience.
- The significant and positive relation between total teaching effectiveness and total attitude towards ICT of college teachers.
- The result also signified the positive and significant relationship was there between the perception of organizational climate and mental health of college teachers based on gender, locality, and duration of the experience. It was found

that male teachers with a favourable perception of organizational climate contributed to a positive mental health condition. On the other hand, female teachers with moderately favourable organizational climate significantly conferred average mental health status. Perception of organizational climate of rural areas had also a significant impact on mental health status. Hence, the teachers concerning 11-20 and above 21 years range of teaching experience who had a moderate level of perception of organizational climate also adversely affect the mental health of college teachers.

➢ There was a positive relationship between total mental health and all dimensions of the perception of organizational climate of college teachers.

➢ The results also indicated a significant positive correlation between the climate setting and their attitude towards the ICT of college teachers for gender, locality, and duration of the experience. The majority of both rural and urban college teachers who experienced a moderate level of the perception of organizational climate had an average level of attitude towards ICT. Move over, regarding the duration of experience with 1-10, 11-20 and above 21 years of teachers with a moderate level of the perception of organizational climate had an average level of attitude towards ICT.

➢ The outcomes also have seen a non-significant but positive relationship between the perception of organizational climate dimensions and three areas of attitude towards ICT of college teachers.

➢ A positive relationship was there between mental health and attitude towards ICT of college teachers for gender, locality, and duration of the experience.

> A positive but non-significant relationship between mental health and all three areas of attitude towards ICT of college teachers also seen from the study.

Based on data analysis, statistical calculations and discussion, it can be concluded that organizational climate, mental health and attitude towards ICT have a significant influence on teaching effectiveness of college teachers. A significant and positive correlation between the perception of organizational climate, mental health and attitude towards ICT with teaching effectiveness means that any increase in these three variables will be followed by an increase in the effectiveness of teacher educators. This restates the importance of these variables in enhancing teacher educators' effectiveness. The present investigation has provided crucial links in the area of teacher education which will immensely help the policymakers and investigators for formulating plans and taking decisions in these important areas. The findings of the present study would be helpful to the planners and policymakers of teacher education in providing a conducive environment to teacher educators so that they may be in a position to give quality teachers to the system and nurturing best talent available to them. The present researcher has investigated a new and contemporary issue of mental health conditions of the teachers which have very many psychological concerns. The link between teaching effectiveness, mental health, organizational climate and attitude towards ICT is not well researched in the north-eastern region of India. That is why research of this kind needs encouragement. As it is the beginning and so could generate new ideas in the field of psychology in future.

The most important attribute of some kind of research is that it promotes a relatively novel idea to the improvement of relevant thesis concerned. Accumulating the concept in mind the researcher has to ascertain some of the informative implications of the study. The existing study is related to the teaching effectiveness, organizational climate, mental health and attitude towards ICT in Assam. This kind of study can be regarded as the first approach in the State of Assam in degree college teachers, as far as the best of the expertise of the researcher.

5.3 *Educational implications of the study:*

Any informative research is beneficial if outcomes into productive educational implications. Before the present analysis is concerned, it can be claimed that valuable evidence has been acquired on the different aspects of teacher effectiveness and its relation to organizational climate, mental health and attitude towards ICT. The following recommendations are based on the major findings of this study and the literature that complements this research.

- ➢ As per the results of the study, there is more effectiveness of college teachers in urban areas in comparison to rural areas. Especially, in rural areas proper attention may be given to a comfortable classroom environment, adequate facilities for implementation of teaching aids in the classroom to make a balance of effectiveness in the college teachers.

- ➢ Efforts may be given to support and give remunerations to fresh teachers so that they can enhance their efficiency and teaching skills. More experienced teachers may be given the required pieces of training to acquaint with teachers of new technological advancement so that they can effectively adopt them in the classroom.

- ➢ It is suggested that the college community may develop infrastructural facilities with proper maintenance of cleanliness and hygiene within the educational campus. Government can also take the responsibility to furnish all the requisite facilities and resources to enhance better performance among college teachers.

- The present study reveals that some portion of college teachers has low mental health. To maintain the physiological and psychological fitness of teachers, it is recommended that yoga and meditation camps may be organized from time to time.

- Urban college teachers had more positive attitude towards ICT awareness than the rural college teachers because of the availability of IT resources in teaching processes. Special technological training programs on ICT may be organised for them and also, appropriate computer labs with internet facility must be installed for SMART classes.

- It was observed from the result according to teaching experience some of the college teachers had a moderate favourable perception of organizational climate at each level. This result suggests that the administrators and principals of colleges must be trained to be more cooperative and helping the new teachers to perceive climate in a better way. It is also much needed to train the management authorities to create an open and congenial environment of the college campus so that the important elements required for healthy living are not neglected. These results will also help the Teachers, Principals, and Administrators to make Organizational Climate better.

- Results exhibited that the Use of ICT by senior teachers was found below. Teachers with limited experience of the new technology in the classroom can be supported by teaming them with teachers (colleagues) who have been successful in

- integrating IT in their classrooms. Innovative e-learning workshops may be intensified to more experienced faculty members to their acceptance of the technology. This will encourage them to make good and frequent use of the internet in their daily duties.
- Other major findings reveal that the teachers having low mental health are less effective in teaching. The mental health of teachers must be properly guided. Special required equipment of the teaching can be ensured by the state or local government for the teachers of an institution. The principals may create general awareness training programs to cope up with the stress management technique and its negative consequences. It would be a better idea if limited workload according to the capacity of the teachers is given to them and special medical care, travelling allowances, special increments and rewards can help improve the overall mental health of the teachers.
- It is recommended that administrators may make an effort by providing an affirmative physical ambience, supportive behaviour with co-workers, freedom for free discussions, to ensure that they carry out educational activities more effectively.

5.4 *Limitations of the study:*

Although the study could give a comprehensive understanding of teaching effectiveness, organizational climate, mental health and attitude towards ICT of college teachers after doing sampling, pilot testing and statistical precision etc., yet the study had some limitations.

These are as follows:

- The area covered for the study was only from two districts [Kamrup (Rural); Kamrup (Metropolitan)] area of the state of Assam. The result would fairly be generalised if more number of districts were selected.
- The study was conducted only on teachers working in the provincialized degree colleges comprising only arts and science stream affiliated to Gauhati University.
- The study was limited to college teachers who are enrolled only in regular mode.
- This study was limited to a small sample only due to scarcity of time, money and human resources.
- The study is limited to four dependent variable teaching effectiveness organizational climate, mental health and attitude towards ICT.

5.5 *Suggestions for further research:*

In the light of the outcomes revealed approximate conclusions from the study, the following suggestions may be considered for future studies;

- To come out with more valid generalizations a larger sample can be taken to provide more diversity and a wider perspective of the research.
- It is recommended to extend the study through engineering colleges, medical colleges, and other professional college teachers.
- The current study did not involve the Principals as well as contractual/guest faculty/adhoc teachers of the colleges. A similar study can be conducted including these persons of the institution from the district to the state level.
- A similar and related topic of research is recommended for future investigations on the other districts of Assam and in other states. The findings of the study need to be corroborated with more dependent variables viz. marital status, personality, and motivation etc. to expand in future studies.

- A study may be replicated between the teachers Government Degree Colleges and the Self-financed Degree Colleges of the State and other parts of the country with the same variables.
- Samples from all districts should be included as there is a scarcity of such studies in the districts as well as the whole state of Assam.
- It will be worthwhile to replicate the study on primary, elementary, secondary teachers, and further the results may be compared to form a comprehensive view on teacher effectiveness.

5.6 Conclusion:

The present study influences to teachers, educational administrators, academicians and others who are related to every domain of education. For the successive acceptance of educational approaches, the effectiveness of the teacher has been pointed out as a critical factor. To attain this kind of efficiency in every aspect of teaching it is essential that every teacher should have high adjustment capacity, staff turnover, positive environmental influence, and a positive attitude in teaching. Therefore, a healthy perception of organizational climate and positive mental health of college teachers have been playing a very important role in becoming an effective teacher. The result based on the study will help create a convenient environment for teaching which may contribute towards the path of teacher effectiveness. It will also enhance the teacher consciousness for creating a provision of a favourable atmosphere for teaching the students. Moreover, it is evident that to cope up with this unique demanding profession, teachers must have a healthy psycho-physiological state of mind which enables them to be adjusted to the realities of their environment. The inference of the present investigation has dragged the attention of experts towards the teacher educators of rural areas. The teachers' mental health is directly related to the work of the classroom. The insufficient psychological services, socio-economic status and government negligence and the stigma for mental health in developing countries are also responsible for increasing mental health issue in citizens. Therefore, it is necessary to establish guidance and counselling cell in all organizations.

It will help to solve the mental, psychological and health-related problems of teachers and students. There is also a necessary step to encourage the use of ICT in classroom teaching. Introduction of ICT in the curriculum should be done mandatory. It will encourage teaching-learning activity. It may be because everyone knows that technology plays a very positive role in the development of teaching and learning. The study contributed a new arena to identify the attitude of technological resources among college teachers. The findings of the study will be helpful for the whole system of education to meet the challenges of changing times. The results will comprehend an information-based foundation for the evolution of future interventions to stop common mental & physical discomforts of aged workers. The best way to prevent moderate mental health conditions is to preserve the stability of organisational culture and impart assistance when executing new technology. It is also predominant aspects to provide specific awareness activities to the middle-aged group through which they can maintain a proper work-life balance. Therefore, we can conclude that mental health, organizational climate, and technology application all are highly correlated with the teaching effectiveness of college teachers. Organizational climate and mental health occupy a very significant place in the life of prospective college teachers. These results will give immense help by contributing to develop a feeling of personal worth for educators.

CPSIA information can be obtained
at www.ICGtesting.com
Printed in the USA
LVHW012115291122
734192LV00014B/538